THE BENELUX COUNTRIES
AN HISTORICAL SURVEY

F. GUNTHER EYCK
Lecturer in History
The American University

AN ANVIL ORIGINAL
under the general editorship of
LOUIS L. SNYDER

D. VAN NOSTRAND COMPANY, INC.
PRINCETON, NEW JERSEY
TORONTO   LONDON
NEW YORK

TO MY WIFE
Courageous Life Companion

D. VAN NOSTRAND COMPANY, INC.

120 Alexander St., Princeton, New Jersey (*Principal office*)
257 Fourth Avenue, New York 10, New York
25 Hollinger Rd., Toronto 16, Canada
358, Kensington High Street, London, W.14, England

Library of Congress Catalog Card No. 59-15097

PREFACE

This volume is in some respects the result of a joint undertaking, just as the Benelux union is the outgrowth —on a much higher level—of a common effort on the part of Belgium, the Netherlands, and Luxembourg. Without the help of many good friends the book might have never been finished, and almost certainly not on time. The author wishes, in the first place, to express thanks to Professor Louis L. Snyder for making this contribution to the excellent Anvil Series possible. His help is very much appreciated. Dr. Anthony Marc Lewis and Dr. Murray G. Lawson to whom this writer is especially indebted gave most valuable advice in the form of penetrating criticism and trenchant observations. Mr. Kenneth E. Colton, Mr. Pierre E. Nys, and Mr. John F. Hostie rendered help on some specific points. Professor Ernest W. McDonnell of Rutgers University not only read the entire manuscript but translated at considerable sacrifice of time the five documents in Part II marked with an asterisk. Professor Fernand Baudhuin of Louvain University kindly read the narrative part and made a number of useful suggestions. Thanks are also due to Professor Arnold J. Zurcher, New York University, who first interested this author in the Benelux countries. Various officials in the embassies and libraries of the three Benelux countries graciously helped whenever called upon. But the partner invariably mentioned last by so many authors and yet the one to carry most of their burdens—the indispensable and indomitable wife—deserves the highest praise for her unflinching help and her sorely tried patience. The present writer cannot possibly make an exception to this rule of final acknowledgment.

The American University   F. GUNTHER EYCK
Washington, October, 1959

TABLE OF CONTENTS

Part I

THE BENELUX COUNTRIES

COMPARATIVE CHART

ERA	BELGIUM			THE NETHERLANDS			LUXEMBOURG		
	POLITICAL	ECONOMIC	CULTURAL	POLITICAL	ECONOMIC	CULTURAL	POLITICAL	ECONOMIC	CULTURAL
Roman (2nd-5th centuries)	Conquest by Romans	First metal, textile, and glass industries	Roman schools established. Christianization	Part-penetration by Romans	Large parts of northern Netherlands uninhabited	Frisian Terp (Mound) civilization	Conquest by Romans	First extraction of minerals	Beginnings of Christianization
Frankish (5th-9th centuries)	Treaty of Mersen (870) divides Lotharingia	Temporary decline in trade	Founding of monasteries (St. Trond)	Absence of strong authority	Fishing and agriculture mainstays of economy	Anglo-Saxon missionaries; first church schools	Division of country as result of Mersen Treaty	Development of agriculture	Founding of monasteries (Echternach)
Middle Ages (10th-14th centuries)	Flanders and Brabant leading principalities	Rise of cities; predominance of Ghent, Bruges, Ypres	Erection of famous cathedrals and town halls	Utrecht, Holland, Gelderland leading principalities	First major dyke system; preservation of herring introduced	Latin, French, and German influences in literature	Ascendancy of House of Luxembourg	Predominance of agrarian economy; first major fairs	Gothic churches built: (Avioth near Orval)
Burgundian (14th-15th centuries)	Control by Dukes of Burgundy	Above cities decline; rise of Antwerp	Humanism. The great Flemish masters	Part-control by Burgundian dukes; northern and eastern provinces free	Rise of cities to prominence (Amsterdam, Haarlem)	Mystics; Brethren of the Common Life; Erasmus	Control of Dukes of Burgundy	First iron furnaces installed	Flourishing of humanism
Imperial Rule: Spanish Habsburgs	Struggle with Spain	Decline of commerce and industry	Jesuits take the lead in education and sciences	Independence from Spain attained	East India Co. formed; overseas expansion	Netherlands largely Protestant. Great Dutch Masters	French and Spanish contest duchy	Decline in population in Thirty Years War	Jesuits prominent in Luxembourg

Eighteenth Century	Austrian absolutism prevails	Mercantilism governs industry	Josephine reforms in religion and education	Decline of the Republic	Dutch overseas trade reduced	"Silver Age" of Dutch culture	Austrian dominancy	New industries. Agricultural reforms	Jesuits maintain centers of learning
French Revolution and Napoleon	Belgian provinces part of France	Abolition of guilds; freedom of Scheldt navigation	French influences dominant	The Netherlands a satellite of France	Dutch trade a victim of the "Continental System"	Popular education developed	Luxembourg a French department	Ending of feudal vestiges	French influences dominant
The "Amalgam" Period 1815-1830	Enforced union with the Netherlands	Dutch support for industrial development	Dutch control of education; religious conflicts	Kingdom of the Netherlands established	Gradual recovery of economy	Revivalism and romanticism	Luxembourg as the XVIIIth province	Neglect of Luxembourg industry	Model schools set up
Later Nineteenth Century	Belgium an independent and parliamentary monarchy	Full industrialization and social conflicts	Flemish national movement. School conflict	Evolution of parliamentary monarchy	Beginning industrialization and social conflicts	"Movement of the Eighties" to deepen art	Struggle for autonomy and independence	Member of Zollverein; railroad network	Luxembourg becomes a center of tourism; influence of romanticism
World War I to World War II	From German occupation to German occupation	War rehabilitation. Great Depression. Van Zeeland plan	Flemish and school conflicts continued	From neutrality to German occupation	Large-scale Industrialization	The "First" and "Second Transition" movements	From German occupation to German occupation	B.L.E.U. established (Belgian-Lxbg. Econ. Union)	Cercle Artistique to develop modern art
Post-World War II	Throne conflict	Benelux Union and European Integration	Gradual settlement of above conflicts	Loss of greater part of empire	Benelux Union and European Integration	Experimentalism	Luxembourg forsakes formal neutrality	Benelux Union and European Integration	Major television center established with Tele-Luxembourg

— 1 —

INTRODUCTION

The Low Countries, more recently called the Benelux countries (Belgium, Netherlands, and Luxembourg), comprise some 25,000 square miles, roughly the size of West Virginia. The population amounts to just over twenty millions. Yet this small region, which has one of the highest densities of population to be found in areas of comparable size anywhere in the world, has played a disproportionately large part in European history. Its location has placed it in a crucial strategic position along the North Sea and Channel coasts. The Low Countries, spoken of occasionally as the key to Europe, lie athwart many of the important roads from east to west and those of lesser importance from south to north. Its extensive lowlands, which rise to a plateau only in the extreme southeast, have always encouraged invasion. Belgium and Luxembourg are especially exposed, since they lack the indented coastline and the natural water defenses of the Netherlands, and from earliest historical times have been the stage for innumerable wars. Celtic, Roman, Frankish, English, French, Spanish, Austrian, and German armies, not to mention the native peoples, have for centuries fought in this region.

In many of its cities and villages hostile forces have clashed on more than one occasion. Neerwinden, for instance, was a battlefield in 1692 when the troops of William III of England and the Netherlands were defeated by the French, and again in 1793 when the Austrians drove back the French. Fleurus was the scene of a French triumph in 1690 and again in 1794. At Guinegate the militia of the Flemish cities won its last great victory in 1479 against the French, while in 1513 the Emperor of the Holy Roman Empire and Henry VIII of England scored here over the King of France. It was Flanders, indeed, which became the bloodiest battleground in Europe and was long considered its most important strategic area. The statement that "he who holds Flanders holds the North Sea" has not been without historic truth. Britain has intervened at least once in each of the past seven centuries to keep any major power from gaining complete control of the Low Countries in general and Flanders in particular. Other European states have gone to war over this area even more often.

Next to the strategic, the economic and political significance of the Low Countries cannot be overlooked. In spite of their physical smallness, their combined volume of trade ranks fourth in the world and one-seventh of the world's trade passes through Benelux ports. First, Belgian cities and then those of the Netherlands were centers of European commerce in the Middle Ages and early modern times. Very recently the Benelux countries have banded together to further the growth of their economies and that of an integrated Western Europe at large. Moreover, these countries have long been in the forefront of the struggle for peaceful international relations, perhaps just because they have experienced war so often. The Dutch capital—The Hague—has been traditionally the seat of the world courts of arbitration. Luxembourg City is the headquarters of the present European Coal and Steel Community. Brussels in Belgium may well become the administrative center of the European Common Market. The Benelux states have likewise greatly contributed to exemplary leadership in their domestic political, social, and economic development. Municipal and regional self-government were widely practiced there before most other European countries benefited from similar institutions. Belgium, the Netherlands, and Luxembourg are nowadays highly developed social democracies and firmly established constitutional monarchies.

Last but not least, the Low Countries have enriched the world with cultural attainments of the first magnitude. Dutch and Flemish schools of painting are held in reverence everywhere. In the sciences, law, and philosophy, as well as *belles lettres*, outstanding and numerous contributions have been made. The Dutch Republic was

the model for religious toleration at a time when the rest
of Europe was still caught up in bigotry. Belgian literature in the nineteenth century stood on an exceptionally
high level. Thus the Low Countries have played a prominent role in the political, economic, social, and cultural
life of Europe, a role all the more noteworthy since it
defied the physical limitations of this region.

This book will not only present the distinguished record but compare the evolution of the three countries.
With the exception of some studies by the well-known
Dutch historian Pieter Geyl, there is—strangely enough
—no work in any language which seeks to compare the
growth of the Low Countries one with another. This
astonishing lack can only be explained by the fact that
these countries have for a very long period of time been
considered as a mere geographic or at best a geopolitical
unit. Their national histories in consequence have always
been treated separately. Yet, the question has been asked
again and again whether these three small countries are
more than a vaguely associated and circumscribed group
of independent rather than interdependent states situated
within a none-too-well defined area. Are these countries
indeed different entities which have been briefly, forcibly,
and abortively joined in one luckless and artificial union
after another, or do they form a natural entity which has
been split asunder by the pressure of external forces? This
question is more than rhetorical and has a real meaning,
especially today when a world trend toward larger political groupings counterbalances the fragmentation of states
and empires due to nationalism. This volume contains
but the most condensed record of the history of the Low
Countries, which nevertheless may help us weigh the relative forces making for unity or diversity among them.

*   *   *

The very term Low Countries has caused much confusion in usage as well as concept. Thus, indigenous
scholars of the eighteenth century referred to Belgians
and Belgica when they meant all of the Low Countries.
Conversely, the Netherlands were referred to as early as
the fifteenth and as late as the nineteenth century as including all of the Low Countries. This interchangeable
use is probably the most interesting evidence of a con-

tinuous though subconscious habit of viewing as a whole
the region between the northern border of France, the
northwestern borders of Germany, and the North Sea.
Further confusion of terminology has arisen from the
fact that Holland is frequently spoken of as if it were to
include all of the present kingdom of the Netherlands,
while in reality it is only one, although the most important, of eleven provinces. Again, the Dutch are occasionally confused in the United States with the Germans,
as in the case of the "Pennsylvania Dutch." Finally, confusion is compounded by the fact that many of the cities
in the Benelux countries have, especially in the border
areas between Belgium and the Netherlands, both French
and Dutch names.

In order to clarify the confusing terminology as much
as possible, the anglicized versions of place names are
used throughout the book. Names of persons are given
in anglicized form when these are generally known and
accepted in English. Less well known names, however,
are given in the native spelling. After the persons of importance in political history, the relevant dates have been
noted when likely to be useful. For rulers, the dates are
given only for the period of their reign. In the case of
scientists and artists no dates are provided, partly in order
to save space and partly because a specific time limitation
has little significance.

The restrictions on space also account for the absence
of any coverage of the Belgian and Dutch colonies. While
the importance that the overseas territories had and still
may have for Belgium and the Netherlands cannot be
gainsaid, developments in the colonies were, except for
economic aspects, peripheral to those in the Low Countries themselves. A final word of apology must be said
about the bare minimum of references to cultural attainments. Here again space was a limiting factor. The em-
phasis in this book thus has been put on political and
social history.

FROM ROMAN TIMES TO THE END OF THE MIDDLE AGES

Roman Times. The recorded history of the Low Countries can be traced back to the era of the Roman Republic. Julius Caesar referred to the Belgae in his *Commentaries on the War in Gaul* and praised this mixed Celto-Germanic tribal confederation for its courage. Some of the component groups of the Belgae were of Celtic stock, e.g., the Menapians in Flanders; but in the eastern and northern parts of the Low Countries German groups prevailed. Many of the tribes, however, were mixed. They included the Nervians between the Scheldt and the Meuse, the Eburons in the later Liége and Limburg areas, and the Trevirans in the Ardennes and near the lower Moselle. The Batavians in the great delta formed by the Waal, Lek, and Rhine and the Frisians still further to the north were entirely Germanic. In the extreme south of the Low Countries, on the other hand, Gallic people were numerous. Romans were settled thinly everywhere between the Meuse and the North Sea.

The population was thus far from being homogeneous, a factor which has always militated against a full union of the three constituent parts of the Low Countries— Belgium, the Netherlands, and Luxembourg. The Celto-Roman-Germanic division took shape as early as the third century B.C. The German tribes, which had so thoroughly obliterated Celtic civilization in other regions, doubtless would have done likewise in the Low Countries, had it not been for the massive concentration of the Celts behind the Coal Wood, the *Silva Carbonaria*. This forest, the western part of the Ardennes mountains, and the Campine marches in the northwest of present-day Belgium are said to have acted as a barrier. Other historians have held that Roman fortifications saved the Celtic remnants. In any event the people to the south of a line running roughly from Dunkirk via Waterloo to Maastricht, and dividing Belgium roughly in half, were known as the Wala—the Walloons. To the north of this divide settled the Germanic tribes. No significant changes have taken place along this ethnic frontier for nearly two thousand years.

Roman civilization introduced for the first time a measure of unity into the Low Countries with the exception of the territories to the north of the great rivers. But the *Pax Romana* was marred by a series of insurrections. As early as 54 B.C. the Eburons and Trevirans rose up against Caesar's legions. Over a century later the Batavi under Claudius Civilis, a native chieftain whose Roman name only has been preserved, staged a large-scale rebellion. Civilis' end is unknown, but the Batavian uprising and that of the Eburons have been extolled for centuries as victories for freedom on the part of stout-hearted natives, proud of their liberties. The common bond of Roman civilization, in turn, has been rather readily forgotten.

The Frankish Period. The Salian and the Ripuarian Franks penetrated deep into the Low Countries by the fourth century. Under Frankish rulers from Clovis I to Charlemagne large parts of the region were unified within the Merovingian and Carolingian kingdoms respectively. But in neither case did this unification persist or really mold the constituent parts into an organic entity. Christianity proved a more effective and lasting means of unification. In the southern regions Christianization was largely carried out by Irish and Frankish priests, while in the north the famous English missionaries Willibrord and Boniface boldly pushed the new faith to the very centers of Frisian paganism and into the desolate wilderness of the bleak moors. Although Boniface was to fall under the blows of untamed barbarians (754), Christian religion and civilization prevailed. A string of fortified places of Christian worship from Tongres to Tournai and Thérouanne in the west and to Utrecht in the north served as unifying and pacifying centers; so too did a number of famed monasteries, including Stavelot-Malmédy, Echternach, and St. Trond.

But politically the Low Countries were far from forming a unit. Their peoples were torn first one way and then

another as the great struggle over the heritage of Charlemagne ensued. The strife between the kings of East and
West Francia, later to develop into the long-drawn-out
conflict of French and German rulers over the *Zwischen-
land* of Lothair I and II—Lotharingia—involved especially the Low Countries. The fateful Treaty of Mersen
(870) cut them virtually in two. Louis the German acquired the eastern parts, while the western regions fell
to Charles the Bald of West Francia. Gislebert, grandson
of Lothair I, shifted his allegiance from the ruler of West
Francia to that of East Francia and vice versa no fewer
than four times. In the end he failed to maintain the
remnants of his powers and possessions.

The possessions were divided into an upper and lower
Lotharingia (Lorraine). Prolonged conflicts ensued between some of its rebellious native dukes trying to recover lost territories and the German emperors who
claimed suzerainty over lower Lorraine. In the twelfth
century the Emperors lost their authority in this region
and the major local princes fought for control over it.
The extreme north and south alone remained outside this
conflict. Flanders became a nominal fief of the French
kings, whose power slowly grew, while Friesland, which
then comprised all of the later Netherlands, north of the
great rivers, remained practically independent. Other territories in the Lotharingian inheritance were contested
by various feudal overlords. Only a common name, Lo-
tharingians, lingered and was applied in the early Middle
Ages to all of the population of the Low Countries. But
this last vestige of unity also disappeared gradually.

The Middle Ages. The causes of union and peace
were hardly furthered by the rise of feudal principalities
in the tenth and eleventh centuries. Since neither the
French nor the German suzerains were strong enough to
assert their authority permanently, the barony established
itself in many instances as the real master. This was particularly true of such border areas as the Low Countries.
In the southwest the Counts of Flanders soon carved out
a very substantial territory, which was divided into Crown
Flanders and Imperial Flanders. The first of these territories was a fief of the Kings of France and the second
of the Emperors. Thus French and German influences
came again into conflict in one of the most important

border areas in Europe and one of its major battle zones.

The Duchy of Brabant, centered on the County of Louvain, became another leading principality. Its realistic rulers, not unlike those of Flanders, transferred their allegiance frequently from the Kings of France to the Emperors, to the English kings and back again to the French rulers. Since Flanders' looms depended on England's wool, however, the Counts of Flanders—though nominally vassals of the French kings—supported more and more often the English monarchs. A third substantial feudal state was the County of Hainaut to the south of Brabant and Flanders. Smaller principalities which strove for recognition and aggrandizement were the Counties of Limburg and Namur. Yet another principality was thickly wooded and sparsely populated Luxembourg. Finally, there existed the independent and powerful Bishopric of Liége, the easternmost region of the southern Low Countries.

These feudal principalities developed more rapidly than those in the northern parts, since they were more heavily populated and more centrally located. The Counts of Flanders, after Baudouin with the Beautiful Beard (988-1035), were especially powerful, since they held a key position which was reinforced by an able administrative organization, territorial acquisitions, and marriage alliances. Their proud slogan was "The first after God." Brabant, too, flourished under the dexterous policies of its dukes and stretched eventually from the river delta in the north to the French frontier. The prince-bishops of Liége enlarged their possessions by shrewd diplomacy as much as by successful wars and managed to outlast many of the great secular princes as independent rulers. Luxembourg remained to the fourteenth century a backwoods area, although it too had some remarkable rulers and possessed natural resources.

The chief city of Luxembourg had been even in Roman times a fortified point of some significance called Lucilinburhuc, "the small fortress." The Counts of Luxembourg enlarged their territory with the support of German Emperors whose loyal vassals they were. Foremost among the medieval rulers of the country was a woman, Countess Ermesind (1196-1247). Although initially left to rule as a minor, she managed to extend her power and possessions by successful marriages. She consolidated her administration, supported the growth of towns by granting charters, and fostered cultural activities by the foundation of new monasteries. The principality came gradually under French institutional influences including the *Loi Beaumont,* which regulated communal rights, and French began to replace Latin at the ducal court. German, on the other hand, remained, with variations, the language of the people. Thus in Luxembourg, too, French and German influences overlapped.

The northern parts of the Low Countries were hardly less divided than those of the south. Holland and Zeeland had yet to establish their preëminence. Much of the attention and energy of the scanty population was absorbed by the unending struggle against inundation. Floods struck almost at regular intervals and reached in 1170 as far inland as Utrecht. Not until the times of Count Floris V (1256-1296) did Holland extend both its borders and influence. Floris penetrated into Friesland to the north and Zeeland to the south. But in international relations he was somewhat less successful. Like so many other princes of the Low Countries, he got entangled in the conflicts between England and France and lost his life by assassination when siding with the latter.

More important than Holland in the early Middle Ages was the Bishopric of Utrecht. Its capital Utrecht was for centuries the only sizable city north of the great rivers and the only urban center of culture. The rulers were energetic and clever churchmen in no way inferior to those of Liége. The *Sticht* or bishopric gradually extended as far north as Groningen. To the west and south conflicts with the Counts of Flanders and Holland limited expansion. Foremost among the secular northern principalities was the County, later Duchy, of Gelderland. Its aggressive princes steadily enlarged their territory and were prominent enough by mid-twelfth century to be seriously considered for the dignity of Emperor. From Flanders to Gelderland sizable feudal states had thus come into being which played an increasingly important part in international affairs and made the Low Countries one of the crucial areas of alliances as well as conflicts.

Rise of the Cities. Noteworthy as the growth of the major principalities was, it soon came to be eclipsed by the spectacular development of the cities. It was this development which not only affected the physical geography of Belgium and the Netherlands but also decisively influenced the national character and history of their peoples. The traditional communal self-government, which later extended to whole provinces, the pride of independence, the practical rationality, the urbane attitude, and the prevalence of the burgher classes in many historical periods and many areas of the Low Countries stem from the growth of the cities. De Tocqueville's observation that "the communes have been for the Belgians the primary school of liberty" may also be readily applied to the Dutch urban centers. City civilization has been the predominant strain in the evolution of the Low Countries.

The origins of medieval cities have been the subject of much discussion, in which the prominent Belgian historian Henri Pirenne (1862-1935) took a substantial part. His central theory is that most of them owed their rise, if not their origins, to the revival of trade in the early Middle Ages. Regardless of the pros and contras of such theories, there can be no doubt that an area of plains and rivers has always favored a concentration of urban localities. Already in Roman times a line of strong points stretched through the southern Low Countries from the North Sea to the Rhine. More cities were added during the Frankish period, but a good number disappeared as the result of the collapse of the Roman Empire and Norsemen invasions, as for example Bavai and Quentovic. On the other hand, such Roman cities as Tongres, Maastricht, and Tournai and such Carolingian additions as Ghent and Bruges survived and became well-known metropolises.

The concentration of cities and towns was heaviest in Flanders, where at the end of the twelfth century over forty municipalities existed. The strategic position of Flanders between France, England, and the Holy Roman Empire promoted the growth of fortified places. The great wool and linen industries likewise must be considered a primary factor in the flourishing of the numerous municipalities. Ghent, Bruges, and Ypres formed a trinity of very influential cities (the Three Members of Flanders) whose powers were not seriously curtailed until the end of the medieval era. The population in each of these three

cities exceeded 50,000. The cities of Brabant, though less
numerous, were hardly inferior in size and power. Louvain, Brussels, Malines, and—since the fifteenth century
—Antwerp vied for leadership with the Flemish cities.
Urban centers could also be found in the Hainaut and
Liége areas. Belgium had indeed become the country of
cities, as Pirenne observed with pride.

The northern towns, on the other hand, developed less
rapidly and did not gain prominence, with the exception
of Dordrecht and Utrecht, until the fourteenth century.
One major cause for their slower growth was that they
were strategically not as well placed; another, that they
were not as populous, since the population in the north
was sparse in comparison with that of the south. Above
all, the northern regions were forever exposed to the
dangers of inundation.

The legal foundations for the growing strength of the
communes were the charters, which in one form or
another were exacted from feudal overlords as opportunities occurred. Huy in the Liége area obtained a
charter as early as 1066. (*See Reading No. 1.*) The
Flemish communes received charters shortly thereafter,
and those of Brabant within the following centuries.
Luxembourg was granted a noteworthy charter in 1244.
(*See Reading No. 2.*) The Charter of Cortenberg (*see
Reading No. 3*) went beyond the purely local guarantees
of earlier documents. It was granted in 1312 by the Duke
of Brabant in return for the recognition of his successor.
The most famous of all charters was, however, the
Joyeuse Entrée (*see Reading No. 4*), which was drawn
up in 1354 by John III of Brabant. Under its terms, which
applied to all cities in Brabant and Limburg, no offensive
war could be conducted, no territory ceded, nor any
treaty made without consent of the subjects. Trade was
to be free from restrictions and subject to legal taxation
only. The ruler, moreover, undertook to abide by the
law of the land.

In spite of such far-reaching guarantees it would be
wrong to assume that the cities of the Low Countries
were the most independent in Europe. Pirenne has rightly
pointed out that the princes retained considerable power
and that the Lombardian cities in Italy, for instance, were
freer from princely influences. Likewise, it cannot be said

that the self-government enjoyed was either originally or basically democratic in character. Certainly up to the beginning of the fourteenth century the communes were under the control of oligarchies. The city council, *collace,* was in the hands of the patricians. It was composed of men with the significant name of *ledichgangers,* those with enough capital not to engage in personal work. In the early medieval trade centers of the Low Countries— the *portus*—the so-called *poorterij* constituted the most important segment of the citizenry. During the development of the guilds, municipal government remained in the hands of the privileged classes through the deans (*dekens*) who headed the corporations. Not until the latter became so numerous in membership that the masses could make their weight felt did a decisive change toward more popular government take place.

Leadership of Flanders.   This change was tied in with a period of general unrest in the Flemish cities, which was of a political and social character. Nobility, foreigners (French), and oligarchs alike were the butt of this unrest. It culminated in mid-fourteenth century and had both domestic and international aspects. The popular party, in which the weavers' guild predominated, banded together as the Clauwaerts, who took their name from the claws of the lion in the coat of arms of Flanders. Their opponents were known as the Leliaerts, those who favored the Bourbon lily and French control. After the bloody Matins of Bruges (May 1302), in which hundreds of Leliaerts were slain, the French and their partisans in the Flemish cities combined to castigate the Clauwaerts.

Much to the surprise of contemporaries, the latter scored a resounding victory when the Ghent militia wiped out an army of French and native knights in the famed battle of Kortryk (Courtrai, July 11, 1302). This Battle of the Golden Spurs, so named from the great number of golden spurs which were picked up by the victorious militiamen, has been immortalized by Hendrik Conscience in the *Lion of Flanders.* The signal triumph gave rise to a new era in the history of the Flemish communes. Bruges and Ypres carried on the struggle, which after several decades merged with the larger conflict between England and France, the Hundred Years' War. It was then that Flanders assumed an importance in the diplomatic struggle which was equal to its traditional role as the main battleground of Western Europe. The leadership in Flanders was now taken by Ghent, which had finally shaken off its Leliaert oligarchy and given full backing to Jacob van Artevelde (c. 1290-1345).

In this remarkable tribune the medieval burgher class in general and the Flemish urban population in particular found an outstanding representative. His major objectives were to keep the Clauwaerts in power, to reduce the influence of the Counts of Flanders, and to conduct a foreign policy which would benefit Flanders, already enmeshed in the Hundred Years' War. He succeeded in bringing about an association of the Three Members of Flanders with Brabant and Limburg. The Count of Flanders had to flee to France, and Artevelde drew ever closer to England, the main supplier of wool for Flemish looms. He even advocated that the Prince of Wales become sovereign of Flanders. Unfortunately, Edward III was less interested in outright alliance than the tribune of Ghent, whose ambitious foreign policies fell short of his aims. Moreover, Artevelde failed to bring about an amelioration of the social tensions in his native city. These were reasons enough to lead to his downfall. The all-powerful guild of the weavers, which had made Artevelde in 1338 the master of the city, was also responsible for his violent death eight years later at the hands of a disgruntled mob.

Ghent continued to be for a long time a center of conflict. Again and again the Counts of Flanders, the Leliaerts, the smaller guilds (which resented the dominance of the weavers), and the French were challenged. In despair the radical weavers even called to leadership Artevelde's son, Philip. But Philip's attempt to emulate the triumph of Kortryk was foiled in 1382 by the French king and the Count of Flanders at Roosebeke. Still Ghent maintained its fighting attitude and rose during the next one hundred and fifty years against such varied rulers as Philip the Good of Burgundy, Maximilian of Austria, and Charles V.

The example of Ghent and Bruges was followed elsewhere in the southern Low Countries. In Louvain a series of uprisings by the underprivileged weavers against the ruling groups took place after 1360. The patricians had ultimately to share the government of the city with the corporations. Liége, too, was not free from a prolonged struggle, fanned by France, between the popular party (*les Petits*) and the aristocracy (*les Grands*). The popular movement in Liége actually occurred earlier than in the other regions. The peace of Fexhe (1316) resulted in a compromise between the urban militia and the warlike Prince-Bishop Adolphe de La Marck (1313-1344). The powers of the ruler were limited and the privileges of Liége and other cities confirmed.

In spite of the protracted clashes between feudal and popular forces and the actual strength of the latter, nowhere in the Low Countries did the communes fully and permanently prevail; nor did they attain quite the power of such city leagues as the Hanse or the Lombardian towns. One major reason for this shortcoming was the intense rivalry and jealousy between individual cities of the Low Countries. Thus Ghent in the early fifteenth century turned against Ypres, and both turned on Bruges. Moreover, there were bitter conflicts between the larger and the smaller cities, which were often dragooned by such centers as Ghent, with a militia of over 20,000 men, into joining the various wars. The cities in the southern Low Countries never possessed an over-all organization, however loose, that could compare with that of the Hanse. Finally, a profound particularism precluded all possibilities for a great association of the urban centers. Common as their interest and development were, they never made common cause on a national scale.

Luxembourg in the Middle Ages.   While the southern and to a lesser degree the northern Low Countries experienced the evolution of communes, Luxembourg developed on different lines. The little principality, with few towns and an agrarian economy, became increasingly important as a feudal state. At a time when such cities as Ghent and Bruges reached their zenith, the House of Luxembourg-Limburg began to rise. In the fourteenth century this dynasty was the most important in central Europe and furnished four Emperors. It was the very smallness of the country which, paradoxically enough, prepared the way for the astounding ascent of the Luxembourg family. In 1308 the Electors of the Holy Roman Empire cast their votes for Henry VII

of Luxembourg in preference to the much more powerful
French candidate, whom they feared.

The new Emperor was probably one of the noblest
sovereigns in medieval times. But before he could assert
himself, he died on a campaign in Italy, whither he had
marched to compel recognition. His son John the Blind
(1310-1346) had become King of Bohemia by marriage.
Although he loved Luxembourg, he visited it only a few
times. His numerous campaigns led him as far as
Lithuania and finally cost him his life at Crécy, where he
fought, though blind, for the French king. It seems a
fitting epitaph that this last royal knight-errant did not
come to final rest until 1946 when his remains were returned, after an Odyssey of centuries, to his native
Luxembourg. Emperor Charles IV, his son, was a very
different man, but he also did not forget his origins. In
1356 he granted a Golden Bull to Luxembourg, which,
like the more famous Golden Bull pertaining to electoral
proceedings in the Empire, was designed to strengthen
orderly administration. But both Luxembourg and the
Empire fell on evil days in the time of the drunkard
Wenzel II. He interested himself so little in Luxembourg
that he pawned it away. His brother Sigismund, who
succeeded him in 1410, did not even bother to visit his
ancestral country once. With his death in 1437 the House
of Luxembourg-Limburg came to an inglorious end.

— 3 —

ATTEMPTS AT REUNION OF THE LOW COUNTRIES

The Burgundian Era. By a strange twist of history
a dynasty which was native to the Low Countries and
yet became progressively more uninterested in its affairs

was followed by a non-native dynasty which concentrated almost entirely on the Low Countries. The Dukes of Burgundy staged within less than a century the most remarkable ascent of any medieval dynasty and one that had profound effects on Belgium, the Netherlands, and Luxembourg. Their glittering successes, against which those of the Luxembourg family paled, were due to a varied policy of diplomacy, intrigue, force, purchase, blackmail, as well as to mere chance. The foundations for the meteoric rise of the Burgundian dukes were laid by Philip the Bold (1364-1404), a younger son of John II of France. By marriage Philip could lay claim to Flanders, Antwerp, and Malines. Having done so in 1384, he realized the advantages of such policies and in the following year brought off a double marriage for his children, John and Marguerite. Apart from these intricate marriage alliances, Philip shrewdly befriended the powerful cities of Flanders. John the Fearless (1404-1419), his enigmatic and choleric son, was primarily interested in the larger contest for the French crown. But owing to his alliance with the English, Flanders' main industries in cloth and linen flourished and the Burgundian provinces in general prospered.

It was in the reign of Philip the Good (1419-1467) that the policies of the Dukes of Burgundy in regard to the Low Countries were most clearly formulated and most fully realized. This cautious, calculating prince with the face of a monk was the first Burgundian sovereign deliberately to conduct a policy designed to revive the Lotharingian kingdom of some six hundred years earlier. The Low Countries were once more to form a unit within the larger *Zwischenreich*. In order to attain his ends Philip steadily enlarged his territories and his influence. In 1421 he bought the County of Namur. In 1430 he inherited Brabant and Limburg. In 1433 he took advantage of the fourth marriage of his famous cousin, Jacqueline of Bavaria, to compel her to yield the counties of Hainaut, Holland, Zeeland, and Frisia, since she had broken her pledge not to marry again. In 1441 he bought title to Luxembourg and in 1455 he established two of his closest relatives as bishops of Liége and Utrecht.

Well might posterity acclaim Philip the Good as

conditor imperici Belgici, the founder of Belgium. Actually his influence reached much farther and he became indeed the "Grand Duke of the West." His son Charles the Rash (1467-1477) rounded out the vastly expanded possessions by the acquisition of Gelderland. At the time of his early death at Nancy the Burgundian state included all of Belgium and Luxembourg as well as two-thirds of the Netherlands. Yet within a generation this powerful duchy disintegrated and the one grandly conceived attempt between the Carolingian empire and the era of William the Silent to unify the Low Countries failed.

The reasons for this failure are in part indicative of the causes for similar failures on other occasions. The Burgundian dukes had not missed the opportunities of introducing unifying elements of administration. The fiscal system was coördinated. The Malines *parlement* served as the highest court. An ambulatory grand council was organized. The provincial estates were continued with the noteworthy addition of the estates-general, through which Philip the Good hoped to gain popular backing. But it was precisely this policy of centralization which caused the most decided opposition of the basic political force in the Low Countries, the communes. Already Philip the Good had been engaged in a running fight with the great cities of the south. The struggle continued in the times of Charles the Rash with a great uprising in Liége. No sooner had the eccentric duke been killed than the pressure of the communes for self-government asserted itself anew. In addition to the failure to win over the cities, the Burgundian state was an artificial creation, not unlike the Kingdom of the Netherlands after 1815. Unification was attempted by unilateral princely action rather than by popular consent. The interests of one part of the realm were uncoördinated with those of another. Thus some of the rising Dutch cities were at war with the Hanse (1438-1441) while their southern counterparts and the rest of Burgundy were at peace. For these reasons the duchy broke apart even faster than it had been put together.

Summary: The Burgundian Era. The three-quarters of a century of Burgundian rule had benefited the Low Countries in some respects. The grave social upheavals and civil wars of the fourteenth century had been ended, as had also, temporarily, the fragmentization into city-states. A more modern and centralized type of administration had been introduced, which in some instances lasted to the eighteenth century. Above all, the era of enforced internal peace had greatly stimulated commerce and art. Although Bruges, Ypres, and to a lesser degree Ghent lost in importance, many of the smaller towns gained. They fell heir to the wool and linen industries, which in order to compete with English production needed a freer development than was possible under the monopolies of the Great Three. Antwerp in particular became the new emporium. Some of the Dutch coastal cities, too, burgeoned with an ever-growing shipping industry. Deventer and Zwolle greatly benefited from the introduction of the preservation of herring in salted form. Other towns such as Leiden and Haarlem became centers of the linen industry.

The golden age of medieval culture in the Low Countries also owed much to Burgundian rule. The famous Gothic cathedrals of Antwerp, Malines, and Breda were rivaled in beauty and grandeur by the town halls of Bruges, Louvain, Ypres, and Brussels. Belles-lettres flourished, but were thoroughly gallicized and influenced by the mannerism of the luxurious Burgundian court life. Philip the Good had perfected the latter with the introduction of the Knighthood of the Golden Fleece (1429). In the fine arts, native talent reached its first pinnacle in the work of such masters as the brothers Hubert and Jan van Eyck, Roger van der Weyden, and Hans Memling. The most famous Dutchman at the turn from the fifteenth to the sixteenth century, was Desiderius Erasmus. This incomparable Renaissance scholar was indeed a cosmopolitan, widely hailed throughout Western Europe; but he was also a native of the Netherlands and represented many of the finest Dutch traits, perhaps more than he was ready to admit. His rationalism, practicality, toleration, internationalism, and humor were Dutch attributes, which Erasmus embodied in a most striking manner. His life and achievements formed a brilliant rainbow against the darkened sky of a much troubled age.

The passing of Burgundian hegemony offered the communes the opportunity to reassert their claims to power. Mary, the daughter of Charles the Rash, was immediately upon her accession compelled by the great Flemish cities and the estates of Brabant and Holland to grant a new charter of liberties. The Grand Privilège of 1477 not only assured the urban centers and provincial estates of their ancient privileges but added new ones. The French king Louis XI also took advantage of the rapid weakening of the Burgundian dynasty and finally invaded the southern Low Countries. In this hour of need the cities of Flanders welcomed support from Mary and her husband, Maximilian of Austria. He was to become the sole ruler when Mary died (1482). Thus began the era of the Habsburgs, which far outlasted that of the Burgundians without attaining its spectacular success.

The Habsburg Rule.   Maximilian, always a stranger in the Low Countries, was soon fighting the cities of the south as so many of his predecessors had done. Yet this time the conflict spread to the north, involving Gelderland and Utrecht. Bruges, in turn, even held Maximilian temporarily a prisoner. Under these conditions it was not surprising that "the Last of the Knights" upon succession to the imperial throne (1493) handed over the regency in the Low Countries to his son. But the latter died unexpectedly; and since Maximilian's son Charles V was only a child, a regent was appointed. This measure initiated the series of regencies which were a specific feature of the history of the southern Low Countries in early modern times and which led to a further strengthening of autonomous tendencies. Such development was particularly favored by the fact that many of the regents were women who attuned their conciliatory policies to the desires of the local population.

The first female regents were Margaret of Austria and Mary of Hungary, who shared between themselves half a century of beneficial rule. The nominal head of the Low Countries was Charles V, who was indeed a native prince, having been born in Ghent (1500). But his manifold duties as Emperor kept him out of the country of his birth. He visited it only five times between 1522 and 1555 when he resigned from the imperial throne. Thanks to the intelligent policies of the regents the Low Countries enjoyed considerable prosperity and stability.

The series of four major wars between Charles V and Francis I, the French king, affected of necessity the lands between the German countries and France. But the Low Countries in the long run gained rather than lost by this struggle. In fact, the southern frontier was strengthened with the acquisition of the Tournaisis and the renunciation by Francis I of his claims to Flanders.

After Charles V had secured the Low Countries against French pressure, a far-reaching reorganization was undertaken. Internal opposition was all but crushed. The quarrelsome Dukes of Gelderland were brought to heel. Ghent, which had arisen once more (1539) in protest against the payment of subsidies, was subjugated by the Emperor, its native son. Henceforth the semi-independent communes existed only in the remembrances of past glory. Full control was also established over Friesland, whose indomitable freemen had long resisted central authority. Overijssel, Drenthe, and Groningen fell likewise to Charles V, who thus controlled all of the Low Countries with the exception of Liége. There remained the task of organizing the various territories in such a way as to assert sovereignty without making it as superficial and ephemeral as in Burgundian times. A number of councils were set up. Brussels became the chief residence. Seventeen provinces were created within the "Burgundian Circle." The *parlement* of Malines was resurrected. But the traditional self-government was not completely discarded and the provincial and general estates were preserved. Well might Charles V hope that he was about to leave to his son Philip a prosperous and homogeneous territorial unit with a balanced government. Yet within a few decades after Charles' abdication (1556) the Low Countries were to break apart again.

The Great Schism. The schism which was to rend the Low Countries so completely asunder was largely conditioned by the great religious upheavals of the sixteenth century. It is of interest to observe that the South rather than the North rallied first to the reform movements. This phenomenon can perhaps be best explained by the facts that the southern regions were more densely populated, that the masses could be more easily inflamed, that a large industrial proletariat suffered from a depression, and that Calvinist influences had penetrated from France and Switzerland. Only in Luxembourg, Namur, and part of Hainaut did Calvinism not prevail. Lutheranism reached Antwerp, the largest city of the Seventeen Provinces, by 1520. Anabaptism sprang up in some of the northern provinces after 1530. Charles V tried to stop the reformers, but neither he nor his successor Philip II could long prevent Protestantism from spreading throughout the Low Countries.

Philip II of Spain inherited with these regions not only the richest and most populous provinces in his vast empire but also an ever-growing unrest. His personality and policies were such as not to hold much promise for an amelioration. Philip's own knowledge of the Low Countries was negligible, his sympathies for its people scant. Above all, his mind was inflexible. Determined to rule the provinces in such a way as to make "heresy" impossible and to spaniardize the government, he utilized all means at his command. In doing so he encountered the specific opposition of the great nobility, which cherished its ancient privileges now in danger of being disregarded.

The nobility, led by the Prince of Orange, William I (1533-1584), and Counts Egmont (1522-1568) and Hoorn (1518-1568), protested on various occasions the highhanded policies of their distant sovereign entrenched in the Escorial in Spain. In April 1566 some three hundred noblemen presented a "request" to Margaret of Parma, the well-meaning regent, for easing religious persecution, ending the Inquisition, and summoning the States-General. It was at this time that the celebrated term *gueux* (beggars) was first used, which afterwards became the epitome of resistance to the Spaniards. A great majority of the nobles adopted the symbols of a beggar's bowl and pouch in the spring of 1566, when still devoted to the king—to whom they swore fealty until ruined to beggar status. There was, however, also the other connotation of *gueux* or *geuzen*, which a courtier had originally given to the term when he referred disparagingly to the remonstrating nobles appearing before Margaret of Parma. Whatever possibilities of compromise existed, they were shattered by the intransigence of Philip. Moreover, an enraged minority of iconoclasts precipitated

further hostile action by Spain when they desecrated
Catholic churches from Poperinghe in the south to
·Leeuwarden in the north. Philip II swore in a rage, "It
shall cost them dear," and dispatched the Duke of Alva.

The Eighty Years' War. One of the first acts of
Alva was the establishment of the Blood Council, which
condemned over 8000 people to death. Its most illustrious
victims were Egmont, perhaps unduly glorified by
Goethe and Beethoven, and Hoorn. The country at large
was held ·to pay a much resented tribute in form of a
5% tax on the transfer of real estate and 10% on the
sale of commodities. Opposition to the Spaniards became
widespread and transcended religious division. William of
Orange, whose realism had led him to flee in time to his
ancestral German possessions, made several abortive
attempts to oust the "bloodhound" Alva. Without the
help of the Geuzen he would have failed altogether.

It was only after 1572 that the northern Low Countries,
specifically Holland—with the significant exception of
Amsterdam—and Zeeland, actively carried on the fight
and laid the foundations for Dutch independence. These
maritime provinces were strategically well placed to become centers of resistance. However inferior the land
forces were as yet against the powerful Spanish *tercios,*
the naval forces more than balanced this disadvantage.
The Watergeuzen in their little boats, who sang "Help
yourself, then God helps you," as they liberated the
coastal towns, acted as the vanguard of militant Protestantism. The war continued in seesaw fashion until the
unpaid Spanish troops ransacked a loyal Catholic city,
Antwerp (1576). This outrage brought Protestants and
Catholics, northern and southern provinces, temporarily
together.

Upon the initiative of William I, always a champion of
tolerance, the *Pacification of Ghent* was drawn up in
1576. (*See Reading No. 5.*) Representatives of all the
provinces except Luxembourg, which was not touched
at all by these momentous developments, agreed to
render mutual assistance, to force the Spanish out of the
country, and to treat the crucial question of religion with
much circumspection. For the first time the Low Countries had voluntarily joined in a confederation and a union

seemed at hand. In September 1577 William I made his triumphant entry into Brussels and was appointed *Ruwaert* (Warden) of Brabant.

It must be regarded as tragic irony that at this very moment new conflicts arose which made a lasting union impossible. Some of the great Catholic nobles intrigued against William the Silent, who they feared was getting too powerful. These "Malcontents" formed an important party in the Walloon regions. The cause of Protestantism was not helped by political or religious excesses, such as in Ghent where a Calvinist republic was proclaimed (November 1577).

Before long the Low Countries were again drawing apart. Diversity had prevailed anew over unity. The French-speaking southern provinces formed the Confederation of Arras (1579). Within three weeks the Calvinist provinces of the north countered by the Union of Utrecht, which in fact created the United Seven Provinces, core of the later Netherlands. The great cities of Flanders still held out on the Protestant side, but circumstances combined to tilt the balance of power soon in favor of Spanish resurgence. Philip II had at last found in Alexander Farnese of Parma a statesman and general equal to William of Orange. Farnese won back by war or diplomacy most of the lost territories, and by 1581 the Protestants were again reduced to an uncertain control of Holland, Zeeland, and Utrecht, as well as a few southern cities.

William I was the soul and symbol of indomitable resistance. His equally resolved arch-opponent Philip II pondered that if only William of Orange could be removed all might yet be well and his authority and that of Catholicism be restored. A prize of 25,000 gold crowns was put on William's head. Several attempts were made upon his life, but he carried on stoically. At last an assassin succeeded in fatally wounding the Stadholder in his Delft residence (July 10, 1584). The life of one of Europe's most high-minded and far-sighted statesmen had come to an untimely end. But his work could not be undone nor his exemplary leadership forgotten. The Dutch had declared their independence while William the Silent was still alive (*see Reading No. 6*) and knew how to maintain it after he had died.

THE DUTCH REPUBLIC, LUXEMBOURG, AND THE SOUTHERN PROVINCES TO THE FRENCH REVOLUTION

Separation of the Northern and Southern Low Countries. The death of the *Taciturne* ended all possibilities of voluntary reunification of the Low Countries. William had even promoted plans to make the Duke of Anjou sovereign of the Low Countries in order to maintain the union. But after his assassination the northern parts were rapidly Calvinized. The south, on the other hand, was in equally comprehensive and compulsory fashion re-catholicized. The northern regions were thus separated from the southern ones by a seemingly unsurmountable barrier. Yet this division was quite fortuitous. It was primarily caused by strategic circumstances and by Spain. Catholicism was no more ingrained in the population of the later Belgium than Protestantism was the natural choice of the Netherlanders. In fact, Overijssel and Gelderland were the most resolute of Catholic provinces during the great schism, just as they were thereafter to become strongholds of Calvinism. Conversely, Antwerp and Ghent had to be forced back into the Catholic fold.

Had the Spaniards been able to cope with the water defenses of the maritime Dutch provinces, or had the English managed to penetrate into the Walloon provinces instead of merely succoring the north, the results might have been very different. As it was, the stronger battalions secured the South for Catholicism and the stronger naval squadrons the North for Protestantism. Unfortunately, there was soon added to the religious division economic rivalry, which intensified the separation. The development of the governmental system, too, followed a different pattern. The United Provinces formed a federation in which self-government on all levels was the core of the institutional structure. In the southern regions monarchical and central authority were fully restored and lasted into modern times.

The Last Phase of the Eighty Years' War. For several generations more the great conflict between the Spanish and Dutch was carried on. The son and grandson of William of Orange continued the war with varying success, as did on the other side the Spanish regents Albert and Isabella. A temporary truce (1609-1621) ended in a renewed struggle, which became part of the Thirty Years' War. The Dutch gained as important an ally in France as they had had in England half a century earlier. Spain exhausted itself and ultimately in 1648 had to acknowledge incontrovertible facts in the Treaty of Westphalia (*see Reading No. 7*). The United Provinces (Holland, Zeeland, Utrecht, Gelderland, Overijssel, Friesland, and Groningen) were recognized as sovereign, while the Spanish Netherlands suffered the restrictions and prohibitions of a lost war. The northern parts of Brabant and Flanders had to be surrendered to the United Provinces. The Scheldt estuary was closed by the Dutch, who thus retained a stranglehold on Belgian commerce. They did not relax it until the French Revolution, and then only temporarily.

The Rise of the Dutch Republic. Having gained national independence and international recognition, the Dutch rose in the seventeenth century to an eminence which seemed hardly commensurate with the smallness of the population or of the country. Part of this phenomenal rise must be credited to the geographic position, which greatly favored the development of maritime enterprise. The boldness of Dutch seamen, the skill of the shipwrights, and the business practices of the merchants were responsible alike for an unparalleled growth in the Golden Century. Amsterdam became the new commercial and financial metropolis of Western Europe. The Dutch navy trebled its ships and by 1650 was twice the size of the combined English and French navies. Dutch explorers had already penetrated before mid-seventeenth century as far as Spitsbergen at one end of the world and Tasmania at the other. With the penetration of the East Indies and the formation of such companies as the East India Company (1602), the Dutch had established themselves as one of the foremost colonial powers. The New World had not been neglected ever since Henry Hudson sailed up the Hudson River and New Amsterdam was founded. The Dutch flag was the only one in the world at that time to fly in five different continents.

Such prominent position naturally invited challenge, which was soon offered by England. The two greatest Protestant sea powers were locked after 1650 in bitter warfare in which Dutch sailors scored resounding victories under such admirals as Maarten Tromp and Michel de Ruyter. England and France, whose conflicts had preserved the Low Countries from domination by a major power for so long, temporarily joined forces (1672). But Dutch water barriers in the southeast and naval activities along the western shores safeguarded Dutch independence as they had already done in the era of Spanish dominance. The sea, the most feared enemy of the Dutch, proved at times in conjunction with the inland watercourses their best ally.

The Pinnacle of Power. The successful war of 1672-1678 led to the greatest triumph of the Republic as a world power. Its new leader, William III (1672-1702), showed himself as clever a statesman as his great-grandfather, William I, as successful a military leader, and even more tight-lipped, while much less warm-hearted. The great alliance formed in 1686 against France was his handiwork. William's unique position after 1688 as king of England and *stadhouder* (stadholder) in the Netherlands enabled him to act as the champion of Protestantism and of the anti-French coalition. Even though he died thirteen years before his inveterate opponent Louis XIV, William III had quietly advanced the international prestige of the Republic in such a way that in the Treaty of Utrecht (1713-1714) it could enlarge its territories by the inclusion of key cities in the southern Low Countries, which otherwise were given to Austria. These cities were henceforth to serve as a land barrier against any further attacks from France. But though the

Dutch thus gained in security, they lost further in popularity with their neighbors to the south, who considered the Dutch garrisons intruders.

Internal Developments. The domestic affairs of the rising republic were of considerable importance to its international situation. The structure of the government allowed for a large measure of regional self-determination exercised through a commercial oligarchy. Not since the heyday of Venice had there existed a more booming and expansionist maritime republic. Unlike Venice, however, the United Provinces were a confederation in fact if not in name. Nominally the seven provinces were equals, but Holland dominated on account of its strategic position, density of population, financial strength (it carried over 50% of the national expenditures), and the tradition of leadership.

The States-General served as the confederate assembly and the only national body of government. But the seven provincial estates were actually more influential, since disputed decisions were referred to them by their delegations in the States-General, where unanimity was required for all actions. Each province had one vote, and the provinces were bitterly divided on many issues. For instance, the maritime provinces had different interests from provinces which were landlocked. The machinery of government was very cumbersome. It was further complicated by the absence of a chief executive. From the death of William I to the seventeenth century there was always more than one *stadhouder* at a time, although the main branch of the Orange family did combine several stadholderships. On the other hand, the "council-pensionaries" of such provinces as Holland and Zeeland were influential officials in their own rights. Conflicts between stadholder and council-pensionary were unavoidable and represented the larger struggle between proponents and opponents of strong central authority.

In 1618 this latent tension flared up when a religious controversy between the Arminians and the Gomarists broke out. The Arminians, who favored a more liberal theology, had as their political leader John van Oldenbarnevelt (1547-1619). This renowned patrician, a close supporter of William I, became the elder statesman after the latter's death. He strongly upheld the "states party" and specifically the interests of Holland to the point of open conflict with the new *stadhouder,* Prince Maurice. A showdown was inevitable when Maurice sided with the Gomarists and challenged Oldenbarnevelt's decision to oppose a national religious settlement in favor of strict Calvinism. Oldenbarnevelt, who had openly advocated resistance by Holland to the orthodox resolutions of the Synod of Dordrecht (1618), was brought to trial and executed.

The struggle between the Princes of Orange and the patricians of Holland was renewed in 1650 and 1672. In the latter year an episode reminiscent of the Oldenbarnevelt affair ended in the death of John de Witt (1625-1672). De Witt was the scion of a Regent family with great influence and on principle opposed to the claims of the Princes of Orange. For nearly twenty years the brilliant but haughty statesman conducted the foreign policies of the Dutch Republic while he tried to undermine the position of the stadholder at home. Had it not been for circumstances beyond his control, such as the alliance between England and France, de Witt might have been the most successful Dutch statesman. As it was, the disaster following the English-French attack in 1672 led to the general acclaim of his chief rival, William III, and the assassination of the great patrician by an infuriated mob, fearing imminent conquest.

In spite of these internal struggles and the apparent weaknesses of the constitutional system, the United Provinces rose steadily in prestige and power. There were several reasons for this phenomenon. The Dutch Republic possessed more wealth than any other European country. The population on the whole was moderate in political and religious matters and composed of freemen, many of whom were moderately well off and skillful in their profession or trade. The leaders, regardless of their views and affiliations, were often men of high principles and a pragmatical approach. The government of the country, however complex, was of a democratic nature unique at that time except for Switzerland. Above all, there was a spirit of self-reliance, progress, and liberty in the land, which asserted itself over all setbacks.

Cultural Attainments in the Golden Age.   Hand in hand with the political and economic growth went a marked cultural ascent. As in the case of the Italian city-states of the Renaissance or the Flemish cities of the fifteenth century, material wealth had its counterpart in great artistic and intellectual attainments. Holland was not only the political and commercial leader of the United Provinces but also the center of the arts. The fullness of life and its enjoyment, the affluence of the burgher class, the secularity of spirit found expression in the paintings of Rembrandt van Rijn, Frans Hals, Jan Vermeer, and other masters. In architecture the Golden Age led to the construction of the beautiful town houses of the Regent families and such town halls as those of Amsterdam and Maastricht. In belles-lettres, on the other hand, a pragmatic people like the Dutch had less interest; and with the exception of Joost van Vondel, the Dutch Milton, no poet gained great renown. In philosophy Baruch Spinoza stood out, and in jurisprudence Hugo Grotius. Both men became victims of a religious intolerance that must appear strange in a country known for its toleration. Spinoza was excluded from the Jewish community for his unorthodox theological views. Grotius had to flee the country as an Arminian. It was in the applied sciences, however, that the greatest abundance of talent could be found, including Hermann Boerhaave, the surgeon; Anton van Leeuwenhoek, the microbiologist, and Christian Huygens, the physicist.

The Southern Provinces. While the United Provinces rose to an unquestioned eminence, the southern provinces underwent a hardly less startling decline. There were several reasons for this spectacular difference of development. In the first place, the southern Low Countries returned tamely to Spanish dominance upon the death of the regents Albert (1630) and Isabella (1633), who had been granted nominal sovereignty by Philip II. The native organs of self-government were subsequently suppressed or much reduced in power. Only in Brabant did the provincial estates preserve some influence. A royal council governed from Brussels, and the provinces were controlled by royal governors. The administration became highly centralized. Pirenne's observation has been very much to the point, that in the seventeenth century the Dutch had a weak central government but a strong national will, while conversely the Belgians had a strong central government but a weak national will.

The southern provinces were further weakened by the series of wars fought on their soil. The Thirty Years' War in its later stages affected the country much. In the five major wars of Louis XIV, it became once more the major battleground of Western Europe. Spanish, French, British, and Imperialist troops alike ravaged cities and countryside. Three of the four decisive battles in the War of the Spanish Succession (1702-1713) were fought on Belgian territory. Far from making common cause with their southern neighbors, the Dutch acted just like any other foreign power seeking its own ends. This became most strikingly apparent after 1715, when the United Provinces closed the Scheldt to all competitive Belgian trade. Antwerp fell rapidly into decline. High tariffs imposed by the Dutch and British further curtailed export possibilities for the Belgian manufacturers and merchants. But the crowning blow was struck in 1727. Commercial interest groups in Ostend and Antwerp had formed the Ostend Company, which intended to trade in the Far and Middle East. But the Dutch, French, and English were so concerned with this possible rival that they compelled the Austrian emperor, who had become the sovereign of the southern Low Countries, to suspend its charter. Commerce, political life, and even the arts became stagnant under such conditions. Only in painting was there an Indian summer of beauty and grandeur with such masters as Peter Paul Rubens and Anthony Van Dyck.

The Austrian Netherlands. By the Treaty of Utrecht the southern Low Countries had been transferred from the Spanish to the Austrian Habsburgs. But the Belgian provinces remained always at the periphery of Austria's interests. Control was chiefly exercised through governors, who at times were very unpopular. On one occasion the Brussels guilds staged a rebellion to regain some of their traditional powers. It was quickly suppressed (1718), and one of the leaders was executed. Not until the end of the eighteenth century did another and far more serious uprising occur. The rule of Maria Theresa in the middle of that century was not altogether unsuccessful or unpopular, although the empress never visited the Austrian Netherlands and would have rather given up these distant lands. They became again the scene of much fighting during the War of the Austrian Succession (1740-1748) when the French undertook a large-scale invasion and occupied much of the country. But by the Treaty of Aix-la-Chapelle (1748) Austria regained control and determined to keep it by increased centralization.

The Brabançon Revolt. Administrative centralization reached its climax during the reign of Joseph II. This most hapless and high-minded of all the enlightened despots saw in the Austrian Netherlands just another of his vast dominions which he wanted to reform. But in his ardor he disregarded completely local traditions and interests. The Belgian provinces were no exception. In fact, it was here that his reform policies caused a revolution—turned against the very reforms themselves. The Emperor had visited these regions in 1781 and thus was the first reigning monarch to set foot there since 1559 when Philip II departed for Spain! But Joseph's zeal led him to misunderstand the desires of the native population. The only effort that could have earned him some gratitude failed when he tried to open the Scheldt estuary (1784). After a brief encounter with Dutch forces he yielded. The Scheldt remained closed. The Emperor was more successful in ending the Barrier Treaty, when Dutch forces gave up the eight fortified places handed to them in 1715; but no specific advantages accrued to the Belgians from this change.

It was in domestic affairs that Joseph II found himself eventually at odds with the populace. He alienated the powerful Catholic clergy by his reforms, which included the dissolution of many monasteries, the permission of mixed marriages, and the Toleration Edict of 1781. More vexing to the country people were such well-meant measures as the regulation of fairs and festivals—the kermesses—which the Emperor tried to reduce to a single day per annum in order to encourage production and discourage drunkenness. Above all, the administrative and judicial reorganizations were widely resented. Such changes could only serve to incite a population which for centuries had stanchly defended local rights and institutions. The ensuing struggle centered around the Joyeuse

Entrée, the great charter of liberties. The Belgians claimed that it was violated in such matters as taxation, and Joseph abrogated it forthwith (1789). But even before the abrogation, tensions had risen to the breaking point. Force was used by the Austrians to compel obedience, and Joseph threatened to "turn Brussels into a desert." Belgian resentment and resistance increased in proportion to such threats and were fostered by developments in neighboring France.

Two political groups formed to challenge Austrian sovereignty. One was led by Henrik van der Noot and the other one by Francis Vonck. Van der Noot, a sly, vainglorious, pompous patrician, was an arch-conservative and aimed at the restoration of the ancient privileges of the southern Low Countries. Vonck was younger, more idealistic, and imbued with the ideas of the French Revolution as well as of the French *philosophes*. The party of Van der Noot was by far the larger and comprised mainly clergy, guilds, and peasants. The Vonckists were supported by the professional and commercial classes and by some of the aristocrats and army officers. Both groups temporarily joined in 1789 against the hated Austrians, who were forced to retreat quickly. Van der Noot entered Brussels proudly in December 1789.

The United States of Belgium. For the first time since the Middle Ages the Belgians were free to choose their own government. (*See Reading No. 8.*) In keeping with the great medieval tradition of regional self-government, a confederation was formed. Under Brabant's leadership a governmental system was devised which resembled, intentionally or unintentionally, the cumbersome institutions of the neighboring Dutch Republic. Foreign affairs and war alone were a joint concern of the confederation, whose only common political body was the estates-general. Black-yellow-red, the colors of Brabant, Flanders, and Hainaut respectively, constituted the new flag. But the confederation stood on shaky legs and even shakier ground. Foreign support was entirely lacking, with the Dutch and Prussians hostile, the British doubting, and the French, in the throes of their own revolution, only mildly interested.

Far worse, however, was the absence of internal unity. The Vonckists challenged the new constitution as being the tool of the "Statists," (the Van der Noot party). The Statists countered these demands by charges that the Vonckists were Francophiles, radicals, and anticlericals. Bad news from Luxembourg, where the Austrians had undertaken an offensive, further incited the conservative peasantry. The Vonckists were proscribed and Vonck himself had to flee to Liége. This development practically destroyed the confederation. Van der Noot's triumph was short-lived. Within a year after his entry into Brussels he was compelled to escape to the Netherlands while the Austrians reasserted their control throughout the country. The Brabançon revolution had failed, but it left behind an awareness of national independence which was to be realized within less than fifty years.

Luxembourg from the Fifteenth to the Eighteenth Century. The history of the principality in this period as well as in later times was very much affected by the same forces and conflicts that made themselves felt in the neighboring countries. During the Eighty Years' War, Dutch and French alike pillaged the duchy. Losses were, however, far greater in the Thirty Years' War, when over two-thirds of the Luxembourg population was annihilated after France entered the fray in 1635. The wars engendered by Louis XIV rolled over the country on several occasions, but French occupation brought certain advantages. Large-scale public construction, including the new fortress at Luxembourg City, created employment as well as profits. Administrative reforms improved the efficiency of institutions.

During the Austrian era the administration was further centralized in the hands of imperial officials. On the other hand, Luxembourgers attained sometimes high rank in Austrian service. Under Maria Theresa the duchy enjoyed a prosperity and a stability similar to those of the Belgian provinces. The iron industry, mainstay of Luxembourg's economy, was gradually developed. Joseph II in turn became even more unpopular in Luxembourg than in the Belgian provinces, especially on account of his anticlerical policies. Yes the Luxembourgers were so conservative that they rejected all thoughts of an uprising against a crowned ruler. Indeed they offered the Austrians a legion to fight the Belgian revolutionaries! But Luxembourgers, Belgians, and Austrians alike were soon thereafter drawn into the vortex of the French Revolution, which was to cause such profound changes in the Low Countries as well as in Europe at large.

Decline of the Dutch Republic to the French Revolution. The spectacular rise of the United Provinces during the seventeenth century stood in stark contrast to a hardly less spectacular decline in the eighteenth century. Rarely has history seen such a complete and quick reversal of position. A number of causes brought about the dramatic weakening of the Dutch Republic. Perhaps foremost among them was the fact that the Dutch had become saturated with wealth and success. They were no longer the bold and dogged fighters who had victoriously withstood the Spanish and the French. The new generations, especially among the patricians, were pleasure-loving and easygoing. Dutch burghers had waxed rich and felt no inclination to risk either their properties or their lives. Even the navy, once the main instrument of the independence and expansion of the United Provinces, fell into decay.

A second major reason for the decline of the Republic was the lack of effective leadership. The traditional struggle between the oligarchs and the Orangists continued unabated with varying results. For more than thirty years after the Treaty of Utrecht and the untimely death of the cousin of William III, the House of Orange went into eclipse. Since there was no immediate claimant to the national stadholdership, the Regents took advantage of the situation. Five of the seven provinces declared for a regime without a stadholder. Most powers were assumed by the provincial or municipal governments. There was no real central authority since the States-General amounted to little more than a composite of provincial delegations.

To make matters worse, no single statesman of the stature of an Oldenbarnevelt or a de Witt arose. Some of the council-pensionaries were not without foresight and realized the dangers of the situation. But even such remarkable officials as Simon van Slingelandt (1664-1736) felt constrained not to alter the existing government. A general assembly of the provincial estates, summoned for the purpose of reform in 1716, failed owing to the particularism of the provinces. Small wonder that the

internal and external strength of the Republic of the
"High Mightinesses" ebbed away. No money was forth-
coming to maintain an efficient fighting force. Corruption
was widespread. The ruling families (thirty-six Regents
in Amsterdam with a population of over 200,000)
monopolized all important offices. In foreign affairs the
Republic held its own as long as Van Slingelandt was alive.
But thereafter the situation deteriorated, and the United
Provinces were a poor starter in the War of the Austrian
Succession (1740-1748). Internal disorders and external
setbacks further weakened the position of the Republic.
William IV was named hereditary stadholder in 1747, but
he lacked the qualities of his predecessors. After introducing some minor administrative reforms he died in 1751,
leaving a minor, a regency, and a much weakened country
behind.

The Regency and William V. During the second
half of the eighteenth century the proud Republic underwent further decline. The regency from 1751-1766 lacked
both appeal and success. Anne, a British princess and
mother of William V, though well-intentioned had little
understanding of Dutch problems. Central authority was
further weakened, as were the armed services. If the
maritime provinces demanded an increase of the navy, the
land-bound provinces requested a strengthening of the
military establishment. In the end neither service was improved, and had it not been for a strenuously guarded
neutrality during the Seven Years' War (1756-1763), the
Republic would almost certainly have been overrun. As it
was, the Dutch gained neither territory nor prestige in this
war. The internal and external situation continued to
deteriorate in the long reign of William V. This last stadholder was slow, vacillating, and helpless. Like Louis XVI
of France, whom he resembled, William V was dominated
by his wife, a Prussian princess.

The final breakup of the Republic occurred between the
American and French Revolutions. The Dutch, try as they
might to stay clear of either, were affected first by the
one and then by the other. It was hardly avoidable that
sympathy would be shown by many Dutchmen for the
struggling American colonists, whose courageous fight
against Britain was quite similar to that of the United
Provinces against Spain. Although the Netherlands

managed to maintain a formal neutrality until 1780, the British took offense at the support the Americans received from the Dutch through such islands as St. Eustatius. Moreover, it became known that American emissaries were in touch with Amsterdam Regents. In the fourth British-Dutch war the ill-prepared Dutch lost all of their overseas possessions. Most of them were restored after 1784, but the vaunted seapower of the Netherlands was irrevocably destroyed.

To make matters worse the latent conflict between the oligarchs and the Orange dynasty revived in new form and intensity. The party of the Orangists, composed of the Calvinist clergy, the artisanate, the peasantry, and the magistrates in the central and eastern Netherlands, was challenged by the party of the Patriots. The latter comprised the upper bourgeoisie, religious minorities, and—for a time—the Regents. It gained the ascendancy and blamed the Orangist camp for all failures. So bitter grew the conflict that the Netherlands seemed on the verge of civil war.

At the most critical moment, William V withdrew to his residence in the countryside, leaving the foundering and disunited Republic to its fate. The Patriots gained control of Holland and made ready for a showdown. At this juncture (July 1787) William's wife Wilhelmina, who resented his weakness, took matters into her own hands. She tried to return to the residence of the Orange family in The Hague but was prevented by the Patriots. Although she was detained by them only very briefly, the incident was greatly played up by the Orangists and their allies, Prussia and Britain. The king of Prussia in fact asked for full satisfaction in connection with the "insult" to his sister. Since this satisfaction was not given, a Prussian army invaded the Netherlands. For the first time since the penetration by the Germanic tribes a large-scale force of invaders had come from the east. Town after town capitulated without a struggle, and within a month Amsterdam was taken. This bloodless war was also the most inglorious ever experienced by the Dutch. It resulted in the restoration of William V and the flight of many Patriots to France. It was from there that they were to reëmerge within a few years in the ranks or train of the French revolutionary armies.

THE LOW COUNTRIES IN THE ERA OF THE FRENCH REVOLUTION AND NAPOLEON

The French Revolution and the Dutch Republic. Long before these armies crossed the frozen rivers to the north (December 1794) the French Revolution had made itself felt among the Dutch. The Orangist Party, strongly entrenched only in the navy, offered little resistance, and soon the Dutch and French forces converged on The Hague. This time the princely couple waited vainly for help. Their Prussian and British allies were in retreat and William V saw himself compelled to act likewise. The last stadholder fled ignominiously to England (1795) and became appropriately the only reigning prince of the House of Orange to be buried in foreign soil. The Patriots, on the other hand, swept triumphantly to victory, although they hardly realized as yet that they were riding the coattails of the French whom their forefathers had tried so hard and so successfully to keep from overrunning the Republic. For twenty years the Dutch were to be tied to France while their erstwhile ally, Britain, became once more a stern enemy.

The Batavian Republic, a satellite of France, was proclaimed. It was so named in the classic tradition, dear to revolutionary France, for the ancient Batavi and their rebellion against the Romans. The Patriot Party, restyled the Unionists, introduced a great number of reforms in order to recast the ancient Dutch institutions in the mold of revolutionary France. But the party of the Federalists, which represented the traditional interests, especially among the remaining oligarchs, resisted. Popular opposition stirred by Jacobin agitators increased, and Dutch radical leaders decided to oust the Federalists. In January 1798 a *coup d'état* was carried out with French connivance, and the Unionists took complete control. A new constitution was devised which ended all provincial autonomy and established a directorate on the French model. But so strong was the tradition of local self-government, and so numerous its supporters that another coup in June returned a more moderate group to power. No further changes took place in either constitution or government for several years. The stolid Dutch, rarely given to extremism, preferred the return to moderation over any radical changes.

Had it not been for the dynamic personality of Napoleon I, the relative stability might have continued without great changes. But in 1801 the imperious Consul demanded more support in men and money. Both had been promised by the Treaty of 1795 in which the Dutch undertook to accept a French army on their soil, to pay a very substantial subsidy, and to surrender Dutch Flanders with several additional towns. When Napoleon ran into some difficulties with the government of the Batavian Republic he reorganized it by the device of a new constitution. This was designed to strengthen the traditional center of power in the country, i.e., the provinces. The antidemocratic tendencies of the future emperor also led him to reduce the franchise sharply. Not until 1806, however, did he determine to end the remaining vestiges of republican government. Napoleon was bent on increasing his family domain as well as his strategic control over Western Europe and determined to make his brother Louis King of the Netherlands. Therefore he presented an ultimatum with the alternatives of annexation or acceptance of his brother. The last council-pensionary gave way and in June 1806 the Kingdom of Holland was proclaimed.

The Netherlands and the Empire. Louis proved himself a ruler more concerned with the welfare of his new subjects than with the interests of the Bonaparte family. He introduced a number of constructive measures. While relations with the Dutch improved, those between Louis and his imperial brother deteriorated. Napoleon was determined to bring his chief opponent, Britain, to defeat through the Continental System, which was to shut out British goods from the European continent. But the smuggling activities of the Dutch, encouraged by the lay of the land, kept Europe's front door ajar, however hard Napoleon and even Louis might try to close it. The emperor upbraided his brother repeatedly to no avail. Not only did British goods filter through, but a substantial British force landed temporarily on Walcheren Island (1802). The French authorities tightened their control to counteract such movements. Eventually Napoleon forced his brother to quit the throne to which he had elevated him only four years earlier. The Emperor lost no time in applying his maxim that the Netherlands "formed by the deposits of three French rivers, the Rhine, the Meuse, and the Scheldt [sic], were by nature part of France." The former kingdom was completely integrated into the empire by 1810.

The majority of the Dutch were at first not strongly opposed to the direct rule of Napoleon. The Emperor was received with much acclaim when he made a triumphant tour through the country. His policies of drastically reducing the interest on the vast national debt proved a boon to financial circles. The administration was streamlined and careers opened to all men of talent. But soon resentment began to mount. Especially objectionable were the Continental System, now strictly enforced, and conscription. Several draft riots occurred, and public opinion hardly got friendlier when of the 15,000 Dutch troops sent to Russia only a few hundred returned. The sharpened censorship likewise served to make the imperial regime more and more unpopular. An ever-growing number of Dutchmen longed for the end of French domination. It was finally to come in 1815. At Waterloo Dutch troops under the Prince of Orange, whose family had been restored to the rule of the Netherlands, fought bravely and victoriously. The Dutch were free again to choose their own government, but a very different state came into existence from that of the Republic which had vanished two decades earlier. Different, too, was the re-emergent Dutch Empire, which had lost the Cape of Good Hope region as well as Ceylon.

The Belgian Netherlands in the Era of French Dominance. The southern Low Countries experienced the influences of the French Revolution and the Napoleonic era earlier than the northern parts. French forces in several invasions submerged the former Austrian provinces. True to their traditional role as Western Europe's major battleground, the Belgian lands became once again a main theater of war. It was there that the first battles on foreign soil were fought by French revolutionary armies as well as the last battle of Napoleon at Waterloo. Already in 1793 the *sansculottes* had penetrated deeply into Belgium, only to be turned back by the Austrians and British. Three years later the Belgian provinces fell completely under the control of France and were incorporated into the French First Republic. As in other satellite countries, France's rule was in part beneficial and in part disadvantageous. Administrative reforms were introduced, civil rights extended, corporations and monopolies suppressed, and the Scheldt was reopened, although Antwerp's traffic actually declined owing to the exigencies of the wars. On the other hand, national self-determination was denied, the country ruthlessly gallicized, Louvain University closed, the refractory clergy deprived of its appointments, and conscription introduced. The latter two measures especially aroused the peasantry. Armed with pitchforks and hunting guns, wearing crosses and white banners, and led by their priests, the peasants ferociously attacked French troops and Francophile Belgians. Although the rising spread from Flanders to the Hainaut, it was quickly suppressed by the French (1798).

The Napoleonic era, which in many ways proved an extension of the revolutionary period, brought few decisive changes. The imperial regime on the whole became more popular because it was less subject to change. Some substantial benefits were derived by those who served as officers or officials. Industry developed on a large scale. The manufacture of armaments flourished at Liége. Industrialized agriculture such as beetroot production helped the peasantry. The Concordat of 1801 pleased the majority of the clergy. Yet in the long run the majority of the population, like that in the other Low Countries, became increasingly restless and finally hostile to the "French sponges" as Napoleon's fortunes ran out. Opposition was strongest in the Flemish regions, where the relief at seeing the end of French dominance was also the greatest. But little did the people realize that in getting rid of yet another foreign rule they were about to be joined to the Netherlands for a period of considerable strain, which would end in revolution.

The Kingdom of the Netherlands. Late in 1813 the Orangist Party succeeded in securing the return of William VI after twenty years of exile. To the shouts of *Oranje boven* (Long live Orange) the energetic and ambitious prince made his entry into The Hague and Amsterdam. But from the beginning of his reign it was clear that he would assume a role different from that of his ancestors. The stadholdership was replaced by the dignity of Sovereign Prince. In December 1813 a constitution was drawn up. It was this constitution, the Grondwet, which became the basic law of the Netherlands and combined traditional Dutch institutions with those of a modern monarchy. (*See Reading No. 9.*) Within a year, however, it had to be revised, since the Netherlands under the provisions of the Vienna treaty system were to include the Belgian provinces. (*See Reading No. 10.*)

William VI, who had become King William I with the assent of the allies, conceived of a United Netherlands long before he returned to the Continent. The fundamental concept of union between north and south had been very strong with William the Silent. The failure to attain union did not mean the end of the idea or of attempts to weld the northern and southern provinces into a unit. In 1632 negotiations for a union had broken down owing to the resistance of such provinces as Zeeland. Some Dutchmen had in turn attempted to divide the southern provinces by joining the Flemish parts with the Netherlands and the Walloon parts with France. Partition of this nature was never entirely discarded in the minds of certain Dutch statesmen and publicists, and neither was the hope to bring ultimately together all regions of the Low Countries. One of the last of the great council-pensionaries, Laurens van de Spiegel (1737-1800), tried during the Brabant revolution to link the United Provinces with the United States of Belgium. But the narrow-minded William V had ruled out all such possibilities. His son, on the other hand, was vitally interested in this issue and left nothing undone to see it settled. Moving quickly and cleverly he persuaded the peacemakers of 1814-1815 to agree to the inclusion of the Belgian provinces in the Kingdom of the Netherlands.

— 6 —

THE ENFORCED UNION OF THE EIGHTEEN PROVINCES TO THE INDEPENDENCE OF BELGIUM AND THE PARTITION OF LUXEMBOURG

The Enforced Amalgam.   While the King was eager and the principal allies willing, the Belgian and Dutch populations felt quite differently on the matter of unification. The Dutch were concerned with the possibilities of Belgian competition on approximately even terms, the ultimate dominance of the larger Belgian population, the prevalence of Roman Catholicism in the south. Many Belgians, on their part, had even more misgivings, the causes of which are indicated below.

But William I was not to be daunted and submitted the revised Grondwet to an assembly of Belgian notables. Their response was thoroughly negative. Of 1603 delegates summoned, 796 voted against and only 527 for it. The remainder abstained or were not present. Most of the opposing vote came from clergy and nobility, while the professional and commercial bourgeoisie were divided. Yet regardless of the outcome, the King, who had the inclinations and abilities of an eighteenth-century enlightened despot, determined to have a union as well as a constitution. By boldly adding 126 votes, which had been cast against the Grondwet on religious grounds, and by the inclusion of the votes of the absentees an artificial majority for the constitution was created. This "Dutch arithmetic" was much resented by the Belgians but gave the king the necessary formal support for amalgamation. The northern and southern parts of the Low Countries— the historic seventeen provinces—were once more joined after an interval of two hundred and thirty-nine years. But the shotgun marriage thus enforced did not augur well for the future.

The new union rested indeed on shaky foundations. Conditions for a successful merger were even less favorable than in 1576. The traditional causes of tension had become more extended and exacerbated. Economic rivalry had intensified with the evolution of Belgian industry, which ranked foremost on the Continent after 1815. Administrative practices and public institutions had come to differ ever more widely. Customs and temper remained as dissimilar in many instances, specifically between the Walloon and the Dutch, as they had been for centuries. Above all, religious issues proved still very troublesome, now that the seemingly temporary division of the sixteenth century had hardened into an apparently insurmountable cleavage. It was over matters of religion that serious conflicts first arose to foil all attempts at full integration of the two main parts of the newly formed Kingdom of the Netherlands. The Roman Catholic clergy, which spearheaded the opposition to union, was much concerned with a possible penetration of Calvinism into the south. The revised Fundamental Law was at once challenged by leading clergymen in a "doctrinal judgment" which inveighed against the religious clauses of the Grondwet. Catholics were exhorted not to take an oath to support it. The government reacted to such provocation, which included the refusal of some clergy to administer sacraments to dying officials. The leader of the clerical opposition was charged with conspiracy against the state and fled the country (1817), only to be condemned to the self-inflicted exile. Thereafter the Dutch administration seemed to have the whiphand.

Growing Difficulties. King William I, like Joseph II, tried to force religious and educational reforms upon a Catholic people. He was especially concerned with education. The so-called royal schools were introduced in Belgium, and in 1822 a law was passed which put all primary-school teachers under the control of the state. This law caused considerable ill feeling on the part of the Belgian clergy. Relations with the government worsened in 1825 when the smaller seminaries were closed and all students entering the priesthood were compelled to take their examinations and degrees at the University of Louvain, which was under state supervision. The Concordat of 1827 did not bring the expected improvement. Rather it was the cause of a further deterioration of relations, since Belgian Catholics charged that the creation of new dioceses in the north, envisaged by the concordat, was deliberately circumvented, while the educational provisions applicable in the south were not withdrawn.

Another major cause of tension was the preference for Dutch personnel in the higher echelons of the government. Under the amended Grondwet the Belgians, who numbered nearly three and a quarter millions as against two million Dutch, were to enjoy equal opportunities. In practice, however, discrimination was much in evidence. Thus only one cabinet minister out of seven, seventeen out of some three hundred high functionaries, one diplomat among twenty-eight, and approximately four hundred officers in a corps numbering over two thousand were Belgians. The only public body where Belgians constituted a majority was the First Chamber, while the Second Chamber was evenly divided between Dutch and Belgian representatives.

The Belgians felt also discriminated against by the distribution of the national debt, which was extraordinarily high for the Netherlands. Although it was twelve times that of the Belgian provinces by 1815, the population of the latter was expected to carry one-half of the national debt. Yet another cause of irritation was the government's handling of the language problem. Dutch was favored by the authorities as the primary medium of communication. But many Belgians were resentful of a language law (1823) which extended the official Dutch language beyond Flanders to Brussels and Louvain. The Walloons who furnished most of the leaders in politics and business always considered French superior to Dutch, and even educated Flemings of that time preferred French.

The differences in the field of economic development were predicated on long-standing rivalries. In this sector

of tensions, however, it was the Dutch rather than the
Belgians who chafed under the *Amalgame*. Dutch merchants and financiers viewed with considerable uneasiness
the growth of Belgian economy. The tariff law of 1816,
which was mildly protectionist, was acclaimed in the
southern provinces but opposed in the north. In 1821
Dutch pressure prevailed and the tariffs were lowered,
much to the chagrin of the Belgians, whose deputies
voted against the new law. Measures of this nature roused
the ire of Belgian Liberals who in the first decade after
1815 had been generally in support of William I on account of his economic and clerical policies.

The Catholic-Liberal Alliance.   The issue that
finally caused the Liberals in Belgium to turn against the
Dutch government involved the freedom of the press.
Several journals of liberal and national tendencies were
founded in the post-Napoleonic era. Among them was
the *Courrier des Pays Bas* in which Louis de Potter
(1786-1859), the sharpest mind among the Liberal leaders, made in 1828 the bold proposal that Catholic and
Liberals henceforth unite in the struggle against the
Dutch. This projected alliance was less unnatural than
appeared at first glance. The Catholic demands for free
education and the Liberal demands for a free press were
quite similar and formed indeed a common platform.

The government's attempt to break up this powerful
new alliance by the imprisonment of de Potter for an
alleged breach of the press law only strengthened the
cause of the allies. Opposition increased and was vented
in two petition movements, which emphasized the demands of both Catholics and Liberals. The king yielded
on minor points, but proved intransigent on the grant of
free education and a free press. De Potter was again
brought to trial and this time condemned to exile (April
1830). Unrest in the country increased. An association
in imitation of the Geuzen was formed, which adopted
as its slogan "Loyal to the king unto infamy." This was
an allusion not only to the Beggars' motto of 1566 but
also to an unfortunate remark of King William I about
the "infamous conduct" of the opposition.

The Revolution of 1830.   In spite of the many
points of friction, several observers in the summer of
1830 did not regard the situation as very critical. It might

have continued for some time with nothing more dramatic than petitions or demonstrations had it not been for the July Revolution in Paris, which affected the political scene in many European countries. Belgium was destined to become "the oldest daughter" of the revolution engendered in France. There was, however, no immediate repercussion of a revolutionary nature in the Belgian provinces. Rather it was a small minority of Francophiles who tried to link Belgian affairs with those of the great neighbor to the south. It was probably this group that originated the broadsheets which tersely announced: "The 23rd of August, fireworks; the 24th of August, celebration of the King's birthday; the 25th of August, revolution!"

While the first two of the scheduled events did not come off as announced, the last one did. Serious disturbances occurred during the night of August 25, 1830. An excited crowd led by students and young bourgeois took its cue from the performance of D'Auber's opera *The Mute of Portici*, which depicted an uprising of the Neapolitans against the French. In truly romantic fashion the audience burst forth into applause and then into action upon hearing such stirring lines as: *Amour sacré de la patrie . . . à mon pays je dois la vie* (Hallowed love for the fatherland . . . to my country I owe my life.) Soon the streets of Brussels were filled with demonstrators who sought out the houses of unpopular officials and destroyed their properties. Such activities frightened rather than encouraged the bulk of the Brussels citizenry, which formed a national guard for the maintenance of order. The country at large was still far from a truly revolutionary spirit.

There was hope for a brief period that a compromise could be worked out, perhaps along the lines of a personal union. Some influential circles such as the merchants of Antwerp were even strongly against separation, which was likely to affect the Scheldt traffic. Ghent was openly Orangist. William I sent his oldest son, the popular Prince of Orange, to Brussels to sound out the leaders of the uprising. But the moderates among them, such as Sylvain van de Weyer (1802-1874) and Felix de Mérode (1791-1857), were soon forced out by radical groups under the leadership of the bold Charles Rogier (1800-

1885), advocate from Liége, and Alexander Gendebien (1789-1869). When the impetuous king was informed by his returning son that the most that could be hoped for was a complete administrative separation under a common crown, William decided to send the Dutch army into Brussels.

Bitter street fighting ensued between September 23 and 27. The defenders of the city were gradually reinforced by contingents of patriots from other cities, foremost among them the men from Liége. But the most conspicuous fighters for independence were the proletarians, who ultimately turned the bourgeois insurrection into victory. On September 27, 1830, the Prince of Orange gave orders for a general withdrawal. The black-yellow-red colors of the Brabançon revolution were hoisted everywhere. A provisional government was established in which Rogier, Gendebien, de Mérode, Van de Weyer, and the returned de Potter figured most prominently. On October 4, independence was proclaimed. The ill-fated union of 1815 had ended in irrevocable divorce due to the incompatibility of the partners. Yet the day was to come, more than a century later, when the two would draw closer than ever before in a *rapprochement* necessitated by common experience.

The Belgian Kingdom. The newly formed state needed above all two things—a constitution and international recognition. The former was debated at length by the National Congress elected by some 45,000 voters in October 1830. From the beginning of its meetings it was clear that both parliament and constitution were to be decisively influenced by the upper bourgeoisie, a development similar to that in France and Britain after 1830. In quick succession the Congress voted the independence of the Belgian people, a hereditary constitutional monarchy, and the exclusion of the House of Orange. The constitution was worked out in some detail and promulgated on February 7, 1831. The document thus drawn up became one of the most advanced and exemplary constitutions of the nineteenth century. (*See Reading No. 11.*)

A far more difficult problem was that of selection of a ruler for the new kingdom. The complications were all the more formidable as the issue was closely linked with the interests of other powers. Especially Britain and France, always much concerned with events in the southern Low Countries, were more anxious than ever, since Belgium for the first time in history had become an independent state. The French, who had actively supported the Belgian revolution from its beginnings, were also the first to take the initiative in the diplomatic activities which followed the formation of the Belgian state. The government of Louis Philippe, while anxious to avoid a general war, was determined to strengthen French influences either by outright annexation, by partition, or by the election of a Frenchman as king of the Belgians. Since the powers were unalterably opposed to the first solution and not willing to entertain the second, the throne candidacy of the Duc de Nemours, a son of the "Citizen-King" was promoted. The Francophile party in Belgium was sufficiently strong to ensure the election of Nemours on February 3, 1831.

At this moment the British government interceded, as could be expected, and a battle royal was joined by such formidable statesmen as Prince Talleyrand and Lord Palmerston. The former favored partition, but Palmerston had promised the Belgians to uphold their newly won independence. With the outcome of the diplomatic struggle much in doubt, the Belgian provisional government appointed a native nobleman as regent. But it became soon evident that the infant state was far too weak to survive in this uncertain form. Orangist and anti-Orangist forces locked horns everywhere in Belgium.

In this emergency the leaders of the so-called independent group, headed by the farsighted Joseph Lebeau (1794-1865), proposed a new candidate, Leopold of Saxe-Coburg-Gotha. This German prince and uncle of Queen Victoria was attractive, clever, and judicious. Above all, he proved acceptable to the parties concerned except Talleyrand. When this astute diplomat finally gave in, Leopold accepted the throne with the proviso that the Belgians would agree to the Eighteen Articles which the major powers had drawn up in London as a possible basis of separation. While these articles were not altogether favorable to Belgium, Lebeau convinced the Na-

tional Congress of the necessity for accepting them. In
July 1831, Leopold made his triumphant entry into Brussels as "King of the Belgians."

The Dutch Counterattack.   But neither Leopold nor
the people over which he was to rule remained undisturbed for long. William I, who had refused assent to the
Eighteen. Articles, decided to restore his position by a
coup de force. Within two weeks after the arrival of
Leopold, Dutch troops crossed the newly established
frontier. This time the Belgians were quickly routed. The
whole struggle for independence might have been in vain,
had it not been for French intervention. It brought the
Dutch advance to a halt, but France in turn withdrew its
troops from Belgian soil only after strong British pressure. An uneasy equilibrium was restored on the basis of
a new set of provisions—the Twenty-Four Articles—
which were less favorable to the Belgians than the earlier
articles. Dutch tolls were reintroduced for the Scheldt
estuary, the national debt of the former Kingdom of the
Netherlands had to be fully shared by the Belgians, border
territories with some fifty localities, including Maastricht,
and half of Luxembourg were definitely lost. The Belgian
government was left no choice but to accept the new
stipulations, which were embodied in the Treaty of London of November 15, 1831. (*See Reading No. 12.*)

The Dutch king, on the other hand, remained adamant.
So far from consenting to the Treaty, William I held on
to the citadel of Antwerp from where the Scheldt estuary
could be controlled. In 1832 Britain and France made
for once common cause in the Low Countries. Breaking
with the Eastern Powers, their partners in the Treaty of
London, they forced the Dutch to quit the important
Belgian fortress. For six more years the Dutch government refused an assent long given by the other powers
in order to legitimize the separation. Then suddenly in
1838 William I accepted the London Treaty because public opinion at home grew increasingly restless over the
unsettled conditions.

Now it was the turn of the Belgians to prove recalcitrant. They had secretly hoped to remain in control of
Luxembourg and Limburg, which they continued to occupy as long as the Dutch rejected the Treaty. With this
opportunity gone, the Belgians thought of armed resist-

ance. But the big powers were unwilling to permit a new conflict. Lacking their support Belgium had to acquiesce. In vain did Gendebien protest "380,000 times" in the name of the populations of Luxembourg and Limburg. In a dramatic vote, with one Luxembourg deputy falling dead from excitement, a narrow majority approved the actual cession of the border lands (March 1839). Belgium and the Netherlands were finally separated for better or for worse, while Luxembourg was unhappily divided. But in this separation lay also the seeds for a closer relationship of independent partners.

Luxembourg from the French Revolution to 1841. As in other phases of its history, the experiences of the Grand Duchy in the early nineteenth century resembled those of its larger neighbors, especially Belgium. During the French Revolution, Luxembourg served first as a base for the operations of allied troops, then for those of the French. The latter imposed heavy contributions, which caused ill feeling. Even more resented were conscription and the confiscation of church lands. Luxembourg peasants, like their Belgian counterparts, took up arms against the French in 1798. The ensuing *Klöppelkrieg,* so named after the cudgels used, ended in the quick rout of the rebels. Henceforth the Département des Forêts was just another French province. The Napoleonic era was first acclaimed, but later became unpopular for the same reasons as in the other Low Countries. Of some 14,000 Luxembourgers who served in the imperial forces, fewer than 5,000 returned. A general economic decline contributed further to the smoldering resentment. Few were those in the duchy who regretted the exile of Napoleon and the passing of French hegemony.

Most of the Luxembourgers welcomed the creation of the new Kingdom of the Netherlands to which their country was joined as the Eighteenth Province. The compromise solution reached at Vienna in 1815 whereby Luxembourg was to be linked as a grand duchy in personal union with the sovereign of the Netherlands was readily accepted. The stipulations that Prussia was to garrison Luxembourg City for the German Confederation, to which the grand duchy was to belong, were likewise not unpopular. But sentiments toward Dutch and Prussians soon underwent decisive changes. The agrarian economy of the country suffered under the industrial and tariff policies of William I of the Netherlands. Taxes were increased although Luxembourg was poorer than either Belgium or the Netherlands. The religious measures of the Dutch government caused even more opposition than in Belgium. Thousands of Luxembourgers emigrated, while those who stayed behind nourished a growing hate for the Dutch. When the Belgian revolution broke out in 1830, many Luxembourgers rushed to its support.

During the following decade the country was subjected to great pressures from all sides. The majority of its citizens favored union with Belgium, but Dutch and Prussian influences prevented such a solution. The London Conference of 1831 proposed at first direct negotiations between Belgium and the Netherlands regarding the future of Luxembourg. After the defeat of the Belgian forces, however, the Twenty-four Articles replaced the Eighteen Articles as the basis for a final agreement. Luxembourg as well as Limburg were to be partitioned. Such a partition was delayed until 1839, when the big powers forced Belgian acceptance, as has been indicated above. Three-fifths of Luxembourg's territory and nearly one-half of the population—mainly Walloon—were ceded to Belgium, while the remainder stayed with the Netherlands. This third partition of Luxembourg[1] reduced the principality to its present size and was responsible for much indignation, which only time could assuage. The Dutch government soon developed policies designed to win the friendship of the Luxembourgers, now that half of their country and all of Belgium had broken away from the Greater Netherlands kingdom.

[1] Luxembourg was partitioned in 1659, when substantial parts in the northeast were ceded to France, and in 1815, when Prussia received smaller areas in the southeast and southwest.

THE GROWTH OF THE KINGDOM OF THE NETHERLANDS

The Netherlands After Separation. The majority of the Dutch were relieved to see the separation finally legalized. Almost at once they set about to improve their domestic affairs, which they had badly neglected while preoccupied with external problems. The primary effort was directed toward a revision of the Fundamental Law. Already in 1840 William I had to agree to reforms proposed by a hard core of Liberals. Much against his will, ministerial responsibility was introduced and other changes made. The King, who was preoccupied with personal affairs involving, paradoxically enough, marriage to a Belgian Catholic, resigned in favor of his oldest son, William II. This easygoing and popular prince found himself soon caught up in the whirls of the revolutionary years 1848-1849. In order to meet public demands and to avoid a revolution, he summoned a constitutional reform committee. The latter, under the compelling direction of the foremost Liberal leader of the times, the scholarly and doctrinaire Jan Rudolf Thorbecke (1798-1872), recommended changes which remodeled the Grondwet on essential points.

The Second Chamber was henceforth empowered to initiate legislation and to approve annual budgets. The First Chamber was to be elected by the provincial estates rather than appointed by the king. The franchise was somewhat extended, but remained based on property qualifications. The principle of direct election was, however, accepted. Civil rights were fully secured. Not until 1866 did a conflict between the monarch and the lower house of the legislature occur. The king and government were challenged by the Thorbeckian Liberals for having

dismissed a minister. The executive branch in turn warned
the voters not to undermine the stability of institutions
by electing opposition members. In the subsequent election, neither side scored a decisive victory, and the near-
equilibrium of forces brought about an involuntary conciliation.

School Conflict.   A second important issue to be
contested in mid-nineteenth century and beyond was that
of lower education. The struggle over it had serious im-
plications and differed from the similar conflict in Belgium only in the degree of intensity. Since the French
Revolution the Netherlands had enjoyed an ever more
comprehensive educational system. It was one of the first
countries to have a separate department of education—
a department whose plans did not remain unchallenged.
The Liberals under Thorbecke's determined leadership
held out for a secular education. But conservative Protestants under the resolute and learned Gulielmus Groen
van Prinsterer (1801-1876), Thorbecke's foremost opponent, favored denominational schools and strict control by the Calvinist authorities. The so-called "neutral
school" was violently opposed by the Conservatives.

A direct clash resulted when the school law of 1857
was passed. It provided for "mixed" or neutral schools
which so appalled Groen van Prinsterer that he resigned
his parliamentary seat forthwith. The struggle was renewed after 1870, when the growing Roman Catholic
population joined the newly formed Anti-Revolutionary
Party to fight the secular school concept. Prolonged party
strife followed, but the Liberal majority in the States-
General held its ground against all attempts to subvert
the principle of the nondenominational public school. Not
until 1889 was a law passed which recognized the right
of state support for "free" schools, where religious instruction could be freely practiced, provided that the
"neutral" schools were equally subsidized. A powerful
combination of Catholics and Calvinists tilted the balance
more and more in favor of denominational education,
and by 1917 an article was written into the constitution,
which made equal support for both types of schools obligatory. Higher education remained largely free from this
controversy, and such Dutch universities as Leiden and
Utrecht remained foremost among European universities.

Social Problems. The most formidable domestic problem was posed by the living and working conditions of the steadily growing class of industrial operatives. Many Dutch people, born to a heritage of "rugged individualism," free trade, commerce, and agriculture as the mainstays of their economy, were unlikely as yet to favor comprehensive and compulsory social legislation. With the 1860's Dutch industry began to expand. In Overijssel and Noord-Brabant, cotton clothing manufacture developed. The coal mines in Limburg were fully exploited, and a ceramics industry was started there. Shipbuilding, now in iron and steel, flourished anew in Rotterdam. But hand in hand with this development went stark social distress. The first regulatory measures were introduced after 1870. In 1874 a child labor law was passed, long after similar laws had been promulgated in several European countries. Fifteen years later another measure restricted hours of work for adolescents and women.

The Netherlands, however, had a long way to go until it became a modern social democracy. In the first decade of the twentieth century accident and invalidity compensation were established, working hours shortened, and long-overdue safety measures in dangerous industries provided. But much of this remedial legislation was adopted only after a series of strikes, not unlike those in Britain, France, or Belgium. The great railroad strike of 1903 was the most severe and could only be broken by massive governmental intervention. On the other hand, the cooperative movement made practically unhindered progress, especially in the countryside.

Concurrently with the growing industrialization, sizable labor movements came into being. Although the revised constitution of 1848 had granted freedom of association, strikes and other collective action on the part of the workers were practically impossible. The restrictive clauses which hampered labor were not repealed until 1872. In the meantime a trade-union movement had got under way with the foundation of the General Netherlands Workers' Association, which professed neutrality in politics and religion. But it was this neutrality which alienated many workmen. Calvinism was still a great force in the country, and Calvinist-minded workers formed their own union, as did also the Catholics, who gradually became more numerous and influential.

The Parties. Socialist action in the political field was left largely to the newly founded Social Democratic League (1881), which was led by a former Lutheran minister with a radical mind, F. D. Nieuwenhuis. This league proposed the solution of social problems by non-parliamentary and extremist means. It was soon challenged by the Social Democratic Labor Party (S.D.A.P.), which was founded in 1894 by the so-called "Twelve Apostles," including a dynamic young lawyer, Pieter Jelle Troelstra (1860-1930). The new Socialist Party, like so many other social-democratic parties, began as an orthodox Marxian party but soon turned in its majority to gradualism and parliamentarism. It was as much concerned with social as with economic reforms and rose quickly in membership and importance. On the eve of World War I it was the second largest party in the country. Its greatest rival in size and in proposals for social legislation was the Catholic Party, ably led by the versatile Monsignor Hermanus Schaepman (1844-1903). It was to assume major importance as the Roman Catholic State Party after 1905.

Among the Protestant denominational parties the Anti-Revolutionary Party was the strongest. It had been founded as a party of reaction to liberal policies, especially in matters of education and religion. Groen van Prinsterer, as one of its spiritual fathers, had stressed the need for keeping the Netherlands a strictly Calvinist country and free from any radical changes. His most noteworthy successor was Abraham Kuyper (1837-1920), whose domineering personality figured prominently on the political scene at the beginning of the twentieth century. "Abraham the Terrible," whatever his shortcomings, was in social questions quite forward-minded and one of the first Dutchmen to realize the importance of winning mass support. On the other hand, his party was to lose the support of the aristocracy, which founded a party to its own liking. The Liberal Party underwent several schisms after the death of Thorbecke. These splits occurred, as they did in other liberal parties, over electoral and social reforms. The orthodox Thorbeckian Liberals refused to underwrite any large-scale reform programs, while the progressive Liberals were invariably among their champions.

The Electoral Reforms.   As in other European constitutional monarchies of the nineteenth century, pressure for an enlarged franchise mounted steadily. The revision of the constitution in 1848 had not resulted in a substantial increase in the number of voters. By 1850 the right to vote was limited to about 13% of all males over twenty-five years of age. This percentage was actually inferior to that of a century before and decreased still further with the growth of population. In 1885 a non-party government introduced proposals for electoral reform, but was blocked by a combination of the Catholic and Anti-Revolutionary parties, which bargained for concessions in matters of primary education. After a narrow electoral victory of the Liberals, the latter passed a compromise measure in 1887 which increased the electorate to some 350,000 out of a total of nearly four million people. "Signs of fitness and social well-being" were qualifying stipulations, as was a minimum age limit of twenty-five years.

The fight for a universal franchise was carried on with increasing vigor, as it was at the same time in Belgium. Universal manhood suffrage was ultimately introduced in 1917 under the impact of World War I. The last of the great Liberal leaders, Cort van der Linden (1846-1935) ensured the passage of an act which not only gave the franchise to all men over twenty-five but promised it to women within two years. Indeed, women received the right to vote by 1919, as did many of their sex in other countries. Proportional representation was also introduced. In conjunction with the electoral law, Van der Linden secured the school law, referred to above, which practically ended the long-drawn-out conflict over education. Thus did the Netherlands just before the end of World War I attain an institutional and constitutional balance which augured well for the further evolution of a progressive society within a parliamentary democracy.

The Arts.   Cultural attainments were not lacking in the nineteenth century, though they did not reach the spectacular levels of the sixteenth and seventeenth centuries. Willem Bilderdijk represented in the Napoleonic era the spirit of conservatism, romanticism, and revivalism. He heralded the coming of the Anti-Revolutionary Party. Only one other author made a similar impact on the intellectual life half a century later—and with very different results. Edward Douwes Dekker, whose pen name was Multatuli ("I have suffered much"), lit with the torch of his brilliant though eccentric mind one of the remaining dark corners in Dutch public life. In *Max Havelaar* he wrote a scathing condemnation of abusive Dutch colonial practices in the East Indies. So strong was his challenge that the Dutch government undertook to enact long-overdue reforms.

But conditions in the Netherlands itself had generally become so acceptable that neither great challenges nor great challengers of a social character arose in the Dutch art world. The one noteworthy exception was Vincent van Gogh, who like Multatuli was a truly revolutionary artist, his whole life a flaming protest against convention. Van Gogh's matchless canvases were hardly in the tradition of the great Dutch masters, which was carried on by such more conventional but gifted painters as Joseph Israels. Evolution rather than revolution, enjoyment rather than sacrifice, had become the order of the day in Dutch life.

The Dynasty. This development was facilitated by a succession of effective and popular rulers. William III (1849-1890) admittedly was antiliberal, but nevertheless in the course of his long reign gave considerable steadiness to the governance of the country. His second wife Emma ruled after his death with intelligence and devotion for nearly a decade. But it was in the reign of her daughter Wilhelmina (1898-1948) that the Netherlands experienced a climax of domestic progress and external prestige that not even the impact of two world wars could shatter.

Foreign Affairs—Relations with Belgium. Ever since the abortive wars against Belgium, neutrality had become an axiom of the foreign policies of the Netherlands, an axiom from which the country rarely deviated. This neutrality, though self-imposed while that of Belgium was internationally guaranteed, served to bring the two hostile neighbors slowly nearer to each other. As early as 1835 the Belgian foreign minister Lebeau stated that "the true destiny of Belgium is to draw closer to the Netherlands." Relations with Belgium underwent a *dé-*

tente after the 1840's. The gradual *rapprochement* culminated in the Treaty of 1863, which ended the obnox-
ious tolls imposed by the Dutch in the Scheldt estuary.
In spite of this noteworthy improvement in relations,
there could be little hope as yet for a collective approach
to international problems and even less for close collaboration in economic affairs.

The liberal Belgian premier Hubert W. Frère-Orban
(1812-1896) negotiated in 1869 for a custom union, but
his ministry fell before any such plan could materialize.
The attempt was renewed after 1880 without results.
Problems of the tariff differential, distribution of receipts
from customs, and protection of Belgian agriculture were
insurmountable at that time, although apparently they
could be solved some seventy years later. Proposals for
an economic and military federation made in 1905 by the
Belgian journalist Eugène Baie were cold-shouldered
by the Dutch. The latter did not share the fears of their
southern neighbors in regard to the new German Empire.
The formation of a joint Belgian-Dutch parliamentary
commission was in vain. In fact, an anti-alliance feeling
became strongest in the Netherlands just prior to 1914
when the Dutch wanted to avoid foreign entanglements
at all costs.

Relations with Other Countries. The neutrality
upheld so scrupulously was rarely deviated from for a
century. Only in a few instances did sentimental reasons
motivate a temporary digression as, for instance, during
the Boer wars. The Dutch quite naturally viewed with
great anxiety the fate of their erstwhile fellow countrymen. The Kuyper government offered its services to
negotiate a settlement before the end of the Great Boer
War in 1901. When the Transvaal president, Paul Kruger,
finally had to flee from South Africa, he was extremely
well received in the Netherlands. Feelings toward Britain
remained unfriendly for a decade thereafter. Britain in
turn viewed with some anxiety the fortification of Flush-
ing. This measure was, however, ultimately counter-
balanced by a bill to fortify the eastern frontiers as well.
Thus a possible defense was prepared against either
Britain or Germany.

The peaceful and neutral intentions of successive Dutch
governments were strikingly demonstrated in 1899 and

1907. Two conferences to maintain international peace were held at The Hague, and although the Dutch sponsored neither of them, they played host to both. Moreover, the Dutch capital housed the first permanent court of international arbitration.

But the touchstone of Dutch neutrality was the relationship with Germany. Doubtless there were deep-rooted sentiments in favor of the Germans. After all, William of Orange had German ancestry and the Orange dynasty intermarried repeatedly with German princes. Moreover, linguistic and economic ties had existed for centuries. At times it did appear as if Dutch governments were leaning in the direction of the powerful eastern neighbor. Charges of this kind were especially made in 1908 when the Netherlands joined the German-sponsored North Sea Declaration, which was to safeguard the territorial integrity of all continental countries bordering that sea. Yet in spite of any pro-German feelings that may have existed the Dutch proved their genuine neutrality when the decisive test of World War I came. The Netherlands maintained a neutral attitude above reproach from any side. By 1919 the country could count its blessings and breathe with relief, having suffered relatively little from the strains and ravages which had been felt the world over and in particular by its southern neighbor.

— 8 —

THE GROWTH OF MODERN BELGIUM TO WORLD WAR I

Belgium, 1831-1918. Though finally separated from the Netherlands in 1831 and different in some essential features, Belgium nevertheless underwent a development in many respects similar to that of the modern

Dutch kingdom. The problems of constitutional revision, social legislation, and primary education, as well as their ultimate solution, were much alike. So were the efforts to keep either country neutral, notwithstanding the failure in the case of Belgium. In addition, the latter country had to struggle with such specific issues as the Flemish question.

Advanced as the Belgian constitution of 1831 had been, it soon proved inadequate as far as its electoral stipulations were concerned. Under the terms of the original constitution, only some 55,000 citizens had the franchise. During the revolutionary years of 1848-1849 some concessions were made, similar to those in the Netherlands and Luxembourg. But no substantial revisions took place. Demands for electoral emancipation continued to be made with increasing vehemence. After 1870 the number of voters rose to 116,000, but this was a small minority in a country with a rapidly growing population. The orthodox Liberals led by the formidable Frère-Orban, who resembled Thorbecke in his influence and policies, opposed a substantial enlargement of the electorate. Yet the movement for universal suffrage under the determined leadership of the doughty Paul Janson (1840-1913) could not be stopped. With the help of industrial labor and some Catholics, Janson pressed for universal suffrage. When his motion for it was defeated in parliament (1893), a series of major strikes broke out. The frightened chamber adopted a compromise measure which gave the vote to all men over twenty-five but also provided for plural voting on the part of those with property or special qualifications. This dual franchise was strongly objected to by the radicals and socialists, who down to 1914 conducted vigorous campaigns for universal suffrage, "pure and simple."

Nevertheless, Belgium had secured a universal manhood suffrage almost a quarter of a century earlier than the Netherlands. Having finally extended this democratic right, the electoral law enforced a corresponding duty, unfamiliar in most countries, by stipulating that henceforth all voters would have to exercise the franchise or be penalized. This law has remained in force to the present day.

Evolution of Parties and Parliamentary Monarchy.
The Liberal-Catholic union, which had done so much to
bring the Belgian state into existence, continued for
some time after 1831. But once the new monarchy had
proved its viability, the alliance began to weaken. Ideological motivations again took precedence over national
considerations. Political coöperation ended by 1846. The
Liberals held a noteworthy congress in which they resolved
to put the educational system under the supervision of the
state, to lower electoral qualifications, and to interest
themselves in social improvement. These resolutions not
only broke up the alliance with the Catholics but also
divided the Liberal Party. Charles Rogier, one of the
heroes of 1831, formed an all-Liberal government in 1847,
and single-party governments remained the rule until
1914. Catholic ministries followed Liberal ones and vice
versa. Thus the great Liberal cabinet of Rogier–Frère-
Orban was in power from 1857 to 1870. Conversely, the
Catholics formed long-lived governments from 1894 to
1914.

Social Conflicts.   Two parties constituted the poles
of the political life of Belgium during the second half
of the nineteenth century. The conflict between Catholics
and Liberals became steadily more embittered and
centered, as in the Netherlands, on the educational system.
To this highly controversial issue there was added the
hardly less explosive social question. The workers in one
of the most highly industrialized countries of Europe
formed until the 1870's a large but ineffective pressure
group. The First International had made some impression
and had drawn into its ephemeral organization such
associations as that of the weavers of Ghent, with their
revolutionary tradition. Some of the men most active in
it were also instrumental in the foundation of the Belgian
Workers Party (1885). Its program was rather moderate,
and even the term socialism was avoided in the naming
of the new party. Among its demands were universal
suffrage, social legislation, abolition of indirect taxes, state
control of public services, and the ending of military duty
by lot. Within ten years after its formation, the Workers
Party became the second strongest in parliament, a record
unequaled in other European countries.

With the growth of a Socialist Party and other labor
organizations, the demand for social legislation grew

apace. Belgian workmen had been exposed to the evils attending the Industrial Revolution from its inception. A royal commission of investigation in 1846 found the over-all situation deplorable. It was especially bad in the Borinage, whose bleak conditions have been strikingly depicted in the early sketches of Vincent van Gogh. But little was done to ameliorate this state of affairs. Under the constitution, operatives did not have even the right of collective bargaining or strikes. Moreover, the invidious method of the workbook introduced by Napoleon I was maintained in order to control the laborer's activities. Only after 1857, when the restrictive labor laws were relaxed, did unions and strikes become more widespread. The Socialist Party and trade-unions kept pressing for long-overdue social legislation. They gained an important ally in the Catholic movement for social reform, which had got under way after the congress of 1863. The groundswell of labor unrest became steadily stronger. In 1886 disorders occurred in such industrial centers as Liége and Charleroi.

Worried by these occurrences and harried by labor organizations, the government prepared the first laws to protect the operatives. Councils of Industry and Work were set up as arbitration tribunals in labor disputes. The nefarious truck system by which workers were paid in commodities came to an end. In 1889 the first regulatory law restricting working hours of women and children was promulgated, fifteen years after a similar law had been passed in the less industrialized Netherlands. Yet Belgium had a far larger industrial population. Furthermore, this piecemeal legislation did not end the demands for more comprehensive and accelerated reform in the political and social fields. Prior to the passage of the universal manhood suffrage act of 1893, violence occurred anew and the country seemed on the verge of renewed social conflict. This was avoided only by a compromise solution and the preparation of more comprehensive legislation. A ministry of labor was created and minor protective labor laws enacted.

But not until after 1900 did the Belgian urban workers enjoy a minimum of protection in the form of workmen's compensation, health insurance, and a weekly day of rest. At about the same time the rural interest groups, especially the small peasantry which constituted the bulk of the agrarian population, organized in the Boerenbond, a very powerful pressure group. Belgian farm holdings were among the smallest in Western Europe, and the peasants stood to gain by collective action.

The School Conflict. A problem which proved as troublesome as the social question was that of lower education. The conflict, similar to that in the Netherlands, centered on the issues of control by state or church and the extent of religious instruction. During the final years of the Liberal-Catholic union a compromise law had been passed (1842). It provided for the coexistence of neutral and denominational schools. But the Liberals were disappointed when over 80% of the municipalities adopted existing Catholic schools rather than create new lay schools. The Rogier–Frère-Orban cabinet asked for additional lay schools in a bill which stirred up bitter controversy. The clergy protested a "scholastic monopoly," but the bill was passed by a strong Liberal majority. Nevertheless it remained a dead letter owing to the resistance of the Catholic hierarchy.

The contest was renewed in 1879 when the Liberal government pushed through a law which established secular schools in each commune, made religious instruction voluntary, and appointed inspectors to regulate all instruction. The clergy, as could have been anticipated, immediately voiced the strongest opposition. The "law of misfortune" was vehemently attacked. In Flanders whole schools were deserted. In vain did the government try to enforce the law by the repression of resistance. Even diplomatic relations with the Vatican were temporarily suspended. An acrimonious "school war" ensued, which was only partly ended when a Catholic government in 1884 revised the Van Humbeeck law of 1879. By 1895 the wheel had turned full circle, with the passage of a new law that established state support for all elementary schools and the compulsory teaching of religion. Unfortunately the law did not increase the number of schools, notwithstanding the fact that 32% of the population were still illiterate. Moreover, the controversy over state subsidies had not come to an end and was renewed as late as 1956.

The Flemish Question. Among the various difficulties that beset consecutive Belgian governments and furthered party strife none were more vexatious and protracted than those existing in the relations of Flemings with Walloons. Geographically the country was about evenly divided between the two ethnic groups. The linguistic frontier halved Belgium by following a line from Dunkirk to Tongres for about 160 miles before turning sharply south into Luxembourg. The Walloons, by temperament more dynamic than the Flemings, held a privileged position in public institutions, although they constituted numerically a minority. The position of the Flemish population deteriorated with the breakup of the unified kingdom after 1831, since Dutch influence was henceforth on the wane. On the other hand, French became the official language, French manners were preferred by the ruling classes, and the French-oriented Walloons assumed leadership in many fields. This development called forth counteraction by some intellectual circles among the Flemish. As early as the 1830's a Flemish national movement had arisen, which was spearheaded by the scholarly Jan-Frans Willems (1793-1846), a stanch Orangist, and Canon Jan B. David (1801-1866).

At first this movement was primarily interested in the revival of Flemish culture, but soon political overtones could be heard. The two segments of the population were sharply divided, although several leaders strove hard to fuse them. In vain did a poet call out: "Fleming and Walloon are only the first names, Belgian is our family name." Unfortunately the rift was very deep and real.

In 1853 the Flamingants drew up a list of grievances. The demands included introduction of Dutch in Flemish schools as well as at the University of Ghent, the division of the army into Flemish and Walloon regiments (commissions were mainly held by Walloons), and the use of Dutch in the administration and the judiciary. This minimal program could hardly be termed excessive in view of the fact that by mid-century there were nearly two and a half million Belgians who spoke Flemish as against one and three-quarter million who spoke Walloon as their native tongue.

Only slowly did successive governments meet some of these demands. Pressure was not as yet extreme, and the leadership in the second generation of the Flamingants was inferior to that in the first. Furthermore, French-

speaking Flemings constituted the social elite, which was
not particularly eager to see Dutch replace French as the
more refined medium of communication. In the 1870's
minor concessions were made in such matters as the
use of Dutch in official proclamations and proceedings in
Flemish areas. But not until 1898 was Flemish recognized
as the second language of the country. A dozen years later
Flemish was accepted as the instructional language in
secondary schools. But by that time the Flamingant
movement had long passed beyond purely cultural issues
and had become an active political force. All-round
equality was demanded ever more vociferously. Attempts
to frustrate these legitimate requests only brought more
bitterness and pressure. Indeed, the day was not far
distant by 1914 when extreme Flemish nationalists, cast-
ing aside the program of the responsible moderates and
patriots, would stoop to coöperation with the German
invaders rather than rally alongside their fellow countrymen.

Belgium on the Eve of World War I.   In spite of
these fundamental problems, many of which were carried
into the inter-bellum period, Belgium was a well-established
and balanced parliamentary monarchy. In some aspects,
such as the universal manhood suffrage and industrial relations, it was ahead of the Netherlands and Luxembourg.
The dynasty was as popular as the ruling families in the
other monarchies of the Low Countries. The longevity of
the Belgian sovereigns added to the stability of the kingdom. Leopold II (1865-1909) did not have the popularity or flexibility of his father. Yet his strong will and
bold vision made him ultimately triumph over personal
and political difficulties. He secured virtually single-
handed the rich Congo region, which after scandals involving the abuse of natives was taken over by the Belgian
state in 1908. On his deathbed Leopold II signed an army
bill, which he had wrested after a long struggle from a
recalcitrant parliament and which introduced personal
military service in place of the substitute system. It was
this new army under the inspiring leadership of Albert I
(1909-1934) that was to play a noteworthy part in
World War I.

But while the country reluctantly girded for the possibility of war and developed at the same time its political,

social, and economic capabilities, cultural accomplishments did not lag behind. In the field of literature, outstanding contributions were made by Flemish and Walloon writers. Among the former was Hendrik Conscience, whose colorful story, *The Lion of Flanders,* glorified Flemish attainments in the fourteenth century. His French-writing counterpart was Charles de Coster, who in *Thyl Uylenspiegel,* the story of the wise fool and practical joker, presented the heroic and turbulent background of sixteenth-century Flanders. By way of contrast, the introvert Guido Gezelle expressed in his refined poetry the spiritual and esthetic values of the Flemish people. The neo-romanticism and mannerism of Maurice Maeterlinck, author of *The Blue Bird,* while far less characteristic of Flemish traits, gained him a far larger audience. In the Zolaistic novels of Camille Lemonnier and the Whitmanesque poems of Emile Verhaeren the industrialized Belgium of modern times found striking expression. It was this aspect of Belgian life which was also depicted in the paintings and sculptures of Constantin Meunier. The tradition of the great Flemish masters was preserved by Hendrik de Braekeleer. In music only César Franck gained world renown.

Belgium in International Affairs, 1831-1914. Belgian foreign policy was predicated upon armed, perpetual, and guaranteed neutrality embodied in the Treaty of 1831. In times of international complications such as the Franco-Prussian War of 1870-1871 or the Moroccan crises of 1905 and 1911, the Belgian governments maintained a scrupulous neutrality. Relations with France were especially delicate. French governments, whether Bourbon, Napoleonic, Orléanist, or Republican, always considered Belgium one of their natural and primary spheres of influence. After attempts at union or partition failed in 1831, the Orléanist government tried to bring about at least a customs union. Their argument was reinforced by the formation of the Zollverein, which likewise made an effort to draw Belgium into its orbit. Under pressure from Britain, which strongly opposed "French soldiers disguised as custom officials" in Antwerp, Leopold I turned down all offers. But with the advent of Napoleon III new complications arose. The Belgians were suspicious of the possibilities of expansionism by the Second Empire.

Relations were not improved by anti-Napoleonic press campaigns which French exiles conducted on Belgian soil. The climax came in 1870, when Belgian forces disarmed French troops trying to escape from the catastrophe at Sedan. Belgium had passed its stiffest test of neutrality yet and proved the validity of this basic attitude in its foreign policy.

The issue of Belgian neutrality was closely linked with that of armaments and a military establishment, since the country had generally recognized the right of self-defense from 1831 onward. But agreement on enlarged fortifications or an enlarged army was difficult to procure. At home large sections of the Catholic and Socialist parties objected to an increase in the armed forces. Conversely, foreign powers such as France and Germany objected at various times to additional fortifications for fear that they might be used by a potential enemy. Germany, especially, followed a policy of alternate cajoling and threatening. In 1904, for instance, William II and Leopold II met, and the Kaiser offered Artois and French Flanders to the Belgians. On the other hand, the Belgian king was threatened with retribution if he did not side with Germany in any future European conflict. Such conduct only strengthened the belief in Belgian circles that it was essential to maintain a watchful and unchallengeable neutrality.

With the deterioration of the international situation, Belgian authorities strove ever harder to build up an army that would give some protection in case of aggression. King Albert was warned repeatedly by his advisers that the "miracle of 1870 would not repeat itself." In 1913 a law was passed, over the opposition of the Socialists, which made military service obligatory as well as general. While Belgium was not willing to make war, it was certainly ready to defend its neutrality.

Belgium in World War I.   The supreme challenge came within a year. The German High Command had long decided to adopt the Schlieffen plan in case of a two-front war. The situation envisaged arose in 1914. Notwithstanding earlier German promises, the Belgian government was presented on August 2 with a fateful ultimatum. (*See Reading No. 13.*) Its courageous rejection (*see Reading No. 14*) led to the inevitable invasion heralded by the German chancellor's historic remark that the treaty guaranteeing Belgian neutrality was just a "scrap of paper."

In spite of staunch resistance the Germans quickly overran the major fortresses and within two months were in control of nearly all of Belgium. Only in the extreme southwest at the Yser did troops under the valiant King Albert hold out tenaciously. It was from that line that the Belgian counterattack, which ended in the liberation of Belgium, was staged four years later. During that seemingly interminable span of time the country was under German occupation, which became increasingly unpopular. Already in August 1914 burning, looting, and shooting had been carried out on a large scale. Louvain's famous library fell prey to deliberate destruction. The activities of the *franc-tireurs* served as a convenient excuse to execute suspected members of the resistance movements as well as hostages.

While this phase passed, a more methodical if less violent repression set in. Patriotic leaders such as the burgomaster of Brussels, Adolphe Max, and the historian Henri Pirenne were either deported or imprisoned. In addition, some 120,000 workers were transported to Germany as forced labor. Public opinion was strictly regimented. Many commodities were requisitioned. Plant machinery was removed wholesale to Germany. The Belgians had to pay a large monthly tribute. Above all, the Germans attempted to divide the Belgian population. The small Flemish Activist movement, which favored collaboration with the occupation authorities, enjoyed German encouragement and even protection. Under the direction of August Borms a Council of Flanders was formed, which prepared for the ultimate separation of the Flemish provinces from the Belgian state. But no deep inroads could be made by the collaborators, whose fellow citizens in the main bravely stood by the existing monarchy. Flemish and Walloon troops joined the general advance of October 1918. On November 22, the King and Queen made their triumphant entry into Brussels. Belgium was again free and sovereign.

But devastation, deprivation, and death were not readily forgiven or forgotten. Forty thousand soldiers had fallen, apart from the hundreds of executed patriots. Nearly a hundred thousand houses had been destroyed, livestock reduced by one-half, and many industrial plants laid waste. One-third of the Belgian population depended on public assistance by 1918. The Belgians rightly considered themselves principal victims of German aggression and insisted on reparations and guarantees. Their attitude was thus quite different from that of their northern neighbors.

The Netherlands During World War I. The Dutch were fortunate during the four and a half years of war in being able to conduct a policy of neutrality, which was denied to Belgium. The major reason was that neither Britain nor Germany wished to see the Netherlands involved. The British feared an extension of German control along the North Sea, while the Germans had no desire to close one of the few remaining open doors through which supplies could be brought in. The Dutch were thus enabled to walk a tightrope and keep from falling into either camp. Yet even their neutrality could not prevent considerable financial and nutritional hardships. Moreover, Dutch maritime trade, including fisheries, was hampered by both British and German naval operations. The Dutch, however, stuck closely to neutrality although they let few opportunities slip by to show their traditional humanitarianism. In 1914 they admitted many thousands of Belgian refugees, while in 1918 they sheltered the fugitive Kaiser.

— 9 —

LUXEMBOURG FROM 1842 TO 1919

The experiences of Luxembourg, erstwhile partner of the Netherlands, were of rather different nature. After the final partition of Luxembourg in 1839, the much reduced Grand Duchy gained in return a measure of autonomy. The Dutch government prepared a constitution which gave to Luxembourg limited parliamentary powers and administrative autonomy. The new ruler, William II, increased his popularity by the dismissal of ranking foreign officials, much resented by the Luxembourgers. But in spite of an easing of the controls, enough opposition remained to cause more demands and even an uprising during the revolutionary years 1848-1849. The Dutch authorities then conceded freedom of the press, constitutional reforms which included a fuller franchise, administrative reorganization, a one-chamber legislature, and the promise of a concordat. The sudden death of William II in 1849, however, left conditions unsettled, and his successor followed a more conservative policy. In 1856 a *coup d'état* reversed the 1848 constitution and strengthened the restored royal authority. The only mitigating feature was the regency of the well-meaning Prince Henry, who gained the confidence of the Luxembourgers. But it was not until the "Luxembourg crisis" of 1867, referred to below, that a decisive change in the constitutional system occurred.

The new and independent Grand Duchy of Luxembourg remained nominally under the Dutch crown from 1867 until 1890, when the death of William III and the lack of male successors made a change in the dynasty necessary. The House of Nassau-Weilburg, a collateral line of the Orange family, assumed the throne of the Grand Duchy. Its new rulers became quickly identified with national interests. The accession in 1912 of the first native sovereign since John the Blind, some six hundred years earlier, was widely hailed. This acclamation was all the more enthusiastic because it was accorded to a woman, the beautiful Marie Adelaide (1912-1919), who hoped to emulate Countess Ermesind, the outstanding ruler in the thirteenth century. The popularity of the dynasty was further increased by the stability and prosperity of the little country. The government was ably led for many years by Paul Eyschen (1841-1915). Among the major reforms introduced were the reduction of franchise qualifications, the secularization of education, and the beginnings of social legislation. Trade-unions became more numerous and powerful, but severe social conflicts were avoided down to World War I.

The Crisis of 1867. The most serious crisis between 1842 and 1914 was political in nature. Yet it was this event which brought an independent Luxembourg into being. Napoleon III had followed the ascent of Prussia to power with growing concern. The breakup of the German Confederation, to which Luxembourg belonged, and the blitzkrieg of Prussia against Austria in 1866 had prompted the French emperor to demand compensation. He asked that Prussia in recognition for French neutrality during the war between the leading Germanic states agree to modifications along the Rhine frontier. Bismarck, who contemptuously referred to a "policy of tipping," officially went along at first with such proposals. He wanted to sound out the French and ensure their neutrality during the conflict with Austria.

Meanwhile Napoleon III prepared to buy Luxembourg from the Dutch king, who was willing to sell it for five million guilders. Just when the instrument of transfer was to be ratified, Bismarck, with the backing of German public opinion, objected, and a Franco-Prussian war seemed unavoidable. At the last moment an international conference sponsored by the Netherlands headed off this possibility. The London Treaty of May 13, 1867, granted Luxembourg independence, which was to be safeguarded by a permanent and undefended neutrality guaranteed by the major powers. (*See Reading No. 15.*) This neutrality was violated concurrently with that of Belgium when German troops occupied both countries in 1914. Thus an ancient community of interests and experiences was restored, which after World War I was to result in an economic union between Belgium and Luxembourg.

THE LOW COUNTRIES
IN THE INTER-BELLUM PERIOD

Relations Among the Three Countries. While Belgium entered into a close relationship with Luxembourg, she passed through an era of marked differences with the Netherlands. These were partly due to the differing experiences in the recent war and partly to the traditional rivalries between the northern and southern Low Countries. Yet in spite of a temporary diversity of views on foreign affairs and a prolonged conflict over the extension of inland waterways, the patterns of development were sufficiently alike to make ultimately possible a *rapprochement,* which was quickened by the economic and political crises after 1931.

Belgium, 1919-1939: Main Problems. To the prewar problems of Belgium, such as the social and educational conflicts and the Flemish issue, were now added those of recovery from four and one-half years of occupation. Recovery put a heavy financial burden upon the Belgian people, who before the war had one of the lowest tax rates in Europe. Modifications in the 1920's introduced, among other changes, an income tax.

But in spite of financial difficulties, various governments pushed further social reforms. Such legislation was undertaken particularly during major crises in order to avoid direct conflict between management and labor. Thus the government of national union at the end of World War I passed laws introducing the first old-age pensions act and the eight-hour day. Under strong pressure from the Socialists, all remaining restrictions on labor unions were repealed. Toward the end of the depression in the 1930's the Van Zeeland government secured minimum salaries, paid vacations, and a forty-hour week in specific industries. The earlier laws concerning women and child labor in industry were augmented and modernized. Nearly half a century of labor legislation had ultimately resulted in the establishment of a social democracy befitting one of the most highly industrialized countries in the world.

The Flemish question, on the other hand, proved most difficult to solve. The attitude of the Flemish Activists during the war had increased tensions. Heavy penalties meted out in the postwar years had done little to assuage feelings. King Albert and the moderate Flemings tried to bring about a fair solution of the unique problem of a majority with a minority status. A language law was passed in 1921 which aimed at linguistic equality, but it took over a decade for this law to become fully operative in all phases of public life. The University of Ghent was finally turned into an all-Flemish institution. Notwithstanding these conciliatory measures, the radical Flemings raised demands for complete separation of administration —the *groote doorsnee*—with the two autonomous parts of Belgium joined under one crown. The "Great Netherlands" idea gained many followers and the Flemish problem acquired a definite political character. The Flemish nationalist party (V.N.V.) more than trebled its seats in the inter-bellum period.

Governments, Parties, and the Constitutional Monarchy. The three-party alliance, which had lasted throughout the war, eventually broke up when the Socialists withdrew from the coalition. In 1925 Emile Vandervelde (1866-1938), their outstanding leader and one-time president of the Second International, formed a coalition government with the Catholics. It was this coalition system that gave stability and even continuity to the chain of governments, of which more than twenty under a dozen different premiers followed one another between 1919 and 1939. Only three major parties, the Catholics—who temporarily lost their majority after nearly four decades—the Liberals, and the Socialists were strong enough to take part in the formation of cabinets or to cause their downfall.

A multiple party system developed, however, after the war. It was originally caused by the influx of new voters after the franchise had been extended to women in 1919, and it expanded with the increased political and economic tensions. The Communist party always remained small, but such Fascist parties as the Rexists gained an ephemeral significance in the thirties. The Rexists were allied with the Flemish extremists, but neither had sufficient strength to overthrow the parliamentary monarchy. Its prestige was on the contrary enhanced by the popularity of the dynasty. Albert I was universally respected and Leopold III, who followed him after his tragic death in 1934, quickly gained general acclaim.

Belgium on the eve of World War II remained a prosperous country with well-balanced institutions, an advanced system of social legislation, and a popular royal house. But all of these assets were soon to be threatened by the expansionist policies of Nazi Germany.

Foreign Relations.   After World War I, Belgium formally ended its neutral status, which had been violated in 1914. Instead, it followed a policy of association with the Allied Powers. In conjunction with them Belgium demanded and received at the Versailles Peace Conference compensation in territory and money. Germany had to cede the Eupen-Malmédy region near the Rhine and Ruanda-Urundi in Africa. A defensive military alliance with France was concluded in 1920. The two countries joined in the temporary occupation of the Ruhr area (1923). A new guarantee of Belgium's frontiers with Germany was written into the Locarno Pact (1925). But within ten years it became evident that Germany was again to be the first military power on the Continent and its most formidable aggressor. King Leopold III returned in 1936 to a policy of neutrality, which was guaranteed by the major powers, only to be broken anew by Germany.

Belgian relations with the Netherlands and Luxembourg underwent far-reaching changes in the inter-bellum period. An economic union with the latter country was concluded in 1921. On the other hand, the Belgians and Dutch were for some time after 1919 on rather strained terms. The Belgians in their quest for security went as far as to claim at Versailles Dutch Flanders and Limburg, thus raising the ghosts of 1831. Nothing came of these demands other than a temporary deterioration of relations. More troublesome and more prolonged was the strain that resulted from the perennial question of inland waterways. On the basis of the Twenty-four Articles of

1831 the Belgians claimed free and equal access to the North Sea as well as to the Rhine. They proposed to construct a canal that was to link the Rhine-Ruhr area with Antwerp and another one from Antwerp to the Waal in the north. Dutch commercial and shipping circles feared undue advantages for their Belgian competitors and exercised pressure against the proposals. Although the Second Chamber in the Netherlands parliament passed the draft treaty in 1925, it was turned down by the upper house. In spite of efforts from both sides no agreement was reached down to World War II, and the two neighboring countries actually took their respective claims to the World Court in The Hague.

On the other hand, the common experiences in the political and economic crises of the thirties led to a *rapprochement*. In 1930 Belgium and the Netherlands joined the Oslo Pact, which required mutual consent of the member states in the matter of tariff increases. Two years later the two countries and Luxembourg concluded the Ouchy Convention, the first direct agreement among the Low Countries on common tariff policies. (*See Reading No. 16.*) Economics became thereafter the primary field of policy coördination. But in politics, too, the three neighbor states drew closer together under the threat of a second world war. On August 23, 1939—the day of the German-Russian nonaggression pact—Leopold III, in behalf of the Oslo powers, made a strong appeal for peace, which Germany answered by the invasion of Poland. Once the war had started Belgium and the Netherlands mobilized for the protection of their neutrality. With the danger of a German attack looming ever larger, the monarchs of the two countries undertook in November 1939 a last call for peace and offered their mediation. (*See Reading No. 17.*) But these efforts remained fruitless, since the Nazis were bent on world conquest. Seven months later the Low Countries were overrun by German armies.

The Netherlands, 1919-1939. The domestic political history of the Netherlands in this period was marked by neither great conflicts nor great changes. Some Socialist-sponsored disorders occurred late in 1918, but otherwise political violence was rare. Constitutional

changes were introduced in 1922 when the right to declare war was transferred from the crown to the States-
General. Further revision took place in 1938 when certain
economic interest-groups were authorized to formulate
regulations of their own. By far the most important
changes, however, were those concerning the franchise
and the party system. At the beginning of the century
only 50% of all adult males could vote. Since 1917,
however, all men over twenty-five have enjoyed electoral
rights. Two years later women were able to cast ballots.
With this substantial broadening of the electorate, parties
began to multiply. By 1929 there existed thirty-seven
political parties, many more than in either Belgium or
Luxembourg, although only nine were represented in the
legislature. The Catholics, who by 1930 composed 36%
of the population, formed the strongest single party.

In spite of the multiple-party system the government
was very stable. There were only three prime ministers
and eight cabinets in the era between the wars. Most of
the governments were right of center and based on a
unique coalition of the Catholic, the Anti-Revolutionary,
and the Christian Historical parties. Such a combination
of confessional parties—the latter two were stanchly
Calvinist—seemed possible only in the homeland of
religious toleration. The Socialists did not attain
ministerial rank until 1939, while the first Catholic prime
minister was installed as early as 1919. The most dominant political personality in the interwar years was
Hendrik Colijn (1869-1944), the formidable successor to
Kuyper as leader of the Anti-Revolutionaries and several
times premier.

Older sources of conflict, such as the elementary-school
struggle, subsided with the introduction of the De Visser
law (1917), which provided for equal support of public
and denominational schools. But other controversies arose
—for instance, over the question of rearmament. This was
opposed by the Catholic and Socialist parties until 1936.
A far more serious threat to the Dutch government
and institutions was posed by the growth of extremist
parties, both Communist and Fascist. Yet the political
maturity and ideological moderation of the Dutch was
such that the overwhelming majority of the people stood

firmly by their democratic traditions. Only the barbarous
onslaught of the Nazis could temporarily disrupt them
after May 1940.

Social Progress.   Social and economic problems
figured on the whole more prominently than the political
ones. As a result of the unrest in 1918 social legislation
was stepped up. The most important enactments of the
time were the Talma Health Insurance Law and the
Aalberse Old Age Benefit and Labor Law of 1919, which
regulated working hours and rest days. A High Council
of Labor was formed in 1927 to advise the government
on problems concerning labor. Industrial councils were
set up by the government in 1933 in order to draw up
collective contracts and work toward conciliation, whenever necessary, of management and labor. Numerous
minor measures concerning social legislation were passed
in the following years and the Netherlands stood in a
fair way to become a full-fledged social democracy when
the war broke.

Luxembourg, 1918-1939.   The closer one moves to
recent times, the more do developments in the Grand
Duchy run parallel to those in the neighboring kingdoms.
Radicalism reared its head in November 1918, just as it
did in the Netherlands. Socialist Luxembourgers even
proclaimed a republic—which lasted for forty-eight hours!
The unpopularity of the erstwhile heroine Marie-Adelaide,
accused of pro-German leanings, served as a rallying point
for the attack on the monarchy. It was quickly restored,
not without French support, when the Grand Duchess
abdicated in favor of her sister Charlotte. A referendum
in 1919 confirmed the new ruler and the strength of
monarchical sentiment.   .

A constitutional revision was carried out in 1919 with
the introduction of female suffrage (as in Belgium and
the Netherlands), proportional representation, and the
principle of popular sovereignty. Social legislation was
likewise augmented. The eight-hour day was introduced
in 1919, but it was not until 1936 that the last restrictions
on labor unions were removed. The 1930's brought a
sharpening of political conflicts, which the government
tried to ease by a projected law curbing extremist groups.
A referendum went against the government (1937),
which gave way to a Catholic-Socialist coalition. The

premiership, however, was retained by the Christian Socialists (Catholic Party) who had held it since 1919. Independence and parliamentarism were upheld, and the centenary of self-government was celebrated in 1939. Within a year, however, Luxembourg was once more invaded and destined to experience its most ruthless occupation.

— 11 —

WORLD WAR II AND THE EMERGENCE OF THE BENELUX COUNTRIES

World War II. None of the Low Countries was spared the terrifying experiences of the Nazi conquest, and each country suffered more than ever before in its history. Belgium and Luxembourg had known earlier German invasions. The Netherlands, however, had been free from foreign control since 1814. The German attack was launched simultaneously and affected the Low Countries in similar fashion. On May 10, 1940, the German steamroller overran Luxembourg. Dutch forces capitulated after five days when Rotterdam was largely destroyed by a terror air raid with a loss of nearly a thousand lives. The Belgian army in turn surrendered after a campaign of eighteen days. There was, however, one significant difference. The Dutch queen, Wilhelmina, and her government carried on the fight from overseas (*see Reading No. 18*), as did Grand Duchess Charlotte. Leopold III, on the other hand, gave himself up to the Germans in order to alleviate, as he maintained, the sufferings of his people.

For over four years the Low Countries bore the yoke of Nazi occupation. Hundreds of thousands of their citizens, including almost all the Jewish population, were deported, and many did not return. Several thousand of those who fought heroically in the various resistance movements fell victim to the occupation forces, as did hundreds of hostages. The Low Countries were systematically deprived of goods and public services. To add ignominy to injury, collaborators with the Nazis were found everywhere. The Flemish Activist movement was revised, and Dutch N.S.B. members terrorized their own countrymen.

Yet the spirit of the great majority of the population in the Low Countries was not broken, however long the much-hoped-for day of liberation was postponed. Belgium was freed in the fall of 1944, but the Netherlands and Luxembourg had to suffer for another eight months. It was in this period that the Third Reich in its death throes inflicted the heaviest damage. The Dutch were practically starved, and Belgian cities were destroyed by V-bombs. Luxembourg was ravaged by the heavy fighting of the winter 1944-1945. Not until 1945 were the three countries free again.

The common sufferings had at least one good effect. The Low Countries drew close together as the result of the traumatic shock of World War II. For the first time in history they formed a voluntary association epitomized in the term "Benelux" (Belgium-Netherlands-Luxembourg).

Belgium, 1945-1959. The foremost problem that Belgium had to face in common with its neighbors was rehabilitation at the end of the war. It is true that Belgian property and production losses were not as high as in World War I. Yet even so, it took months before life returned to some degree of normality. Probably the most galling issue was the weeding out of collaborators and their punishment. No fewer than 53,000 condemnations were pronounced. Of these, 30,000 pertained to Flemings, about 14,000 to Walloons, and 9,000 to the mixed Brabant (Brussels) region. Some 250 death sentences were carried out, although the number of those subject to the capital penalty was much greater. As time went by, many of the sentences were reduced. Yet collaboration had left its ugly mark and could not be forgotten, even when forgiven.

The most controversial case to arise from the charges of collaboration was that of the King himself. After the Normandy landings of the Allies, he had been removed as a prisoner to Germany. When he wanted to return in 1945, it became evident that no hero's return awaited him. In fact a major political crisis was in the making, which shook Belgium to its foundations. The country was split between those who opposed a return of the hapless King and those who favored his restoration. In March 1950 a referendum showed that a narrow majority of Belgians were willing to accept Leopold III again as king. But only in the Flemish parts did a sufficient plurality of affirmative votes exist. The situation was further complicated by the sudden arrival of the monarch in Belgium. Protestations occurred everywhere, and civil war seemed possible. Under strong pressure Leopold III finally consented to transfer his royal powers to Prince Baudouin. (*See Reading No. 19.*) The latter became king twelve months later (July 1951) when his father formally abdicated.

The traditional struggle between Walloons and Flemings had again manifested itself during the controversy over Leopold. It was also to show itself in other forms. After the Flemish people gained formal equality, it was the turn of the Walloons to complain about discrimination. By 1950 only 35% of the population was Walloon as against 50% Flemish, with the rest about evenly divided in the Brussels *arrondissement*. A proposal to establish a federal organization of the kingdom in order to safeguard Walloon interests was decisively defeated in parliament. Flemish complaints could also be frequently heard on such issues as preference for Walloons in the higher bureaucracy, a larger percentage of Flemish unemployed, and inadequate application of the language laws. While claims and counterclaims are thus made, no definite rift between the two population groups is likely to occur. On the contrary, the work of such institutions as the Harmel Center, which conducts objective studies and encourages cooperation, may ultimately lead to a satisfactory *modus vivendi*.

Another issue of long standing, the school problem, has

recently proved to be more explosive. After several decades of comparative lull, a Socialist-Liberal bill to
erect additional public schools and to cut subsidies for
parochial schools by 15% caused widespread opposition.
Rioting took place in 1955, but the bill was passed in the
absence of the deputies of the Catholic Party. Not until
1958 did the excitement die down when a tripartite commission worked out a formula which gives equal support
to public and parochial schools.

In social legislation Belgium has made considerable
headway since 1945. The country developed one of the
highest standards of living in Europe, and in social
security expenditures led all other European countries.
Belgium has also been the first country to set up a ministry
for the middle classes. Labor interests are likewise given
much attention. The 45-hour week in basic industries
was introduced in 1957. Labor-management councils have
played an increasingly important part in the settlement
of disputes, although strikes, such as the great metal-
worker strike of 1957, still occur. One persistent problem
is to find the necessary labor force in certain industries,
such as mining, where a good number of foreigners are
employed.

The Netherlands, 1945-1959. While the immediate postwar difficulties in Belgium were mainly of a
political nature, those of its northern neighbor were
primarily economic. Destruction had been more widespread than in the other parts of the Low Countries. The
Netherlands had been thoroughly ravished and its population nearly famished as the result of Nazi occupation.
Almost 250,000 people had been killed or had died of
famine. Much of the land laboriously reclaimed had been
inundated. Industry had been thoroughly despoiled. But
the Dutch struggled heroically and successfully for
economic rehabilitation.

Next to this spectacular recovery, land reclamation
produced the greatest success for the Dutch. The thousand
years' fight against inundation (over half the population
live below sea level) is carried on with more determination than ever. Even though the unrelenting sea made one
of its most devastating assaults in January 1953, the
people refused to yield. In the same year 119,000 acres
that had been wrested from the waters of the Zuider

Zee were opened to farming. The impoldering (drying out) of much of this sea will ultimately add some 10% to the arable parts of the Netherlands. A still greater scheme is the Delta Plan, which is to establish flood controls throughout Zeeland. The Dutch can indeed quote today with more justification than ever the famous saying "God created the world, but the Dutch created Holland." By way of comparison, other current developments outside the economic sphere seem relatively unimportant.

No dramatic events have shaken the political peace or the constitutional balance of the country since the punishment of the war criminals.[1] From 1948 when Queen Juliana took her mother's place upon the retirement of the latter after fifty years of exemplary service, the government was headed by a single premier until December 1958. Willem Drees (b. 1886), the quiet leader of the Socialist Party, now restyled Labor Party because it wants to transcend the narrow confines of Marxism, proved to be an able statesman. His task was eased by the fact that the various cabinets under him were formed by coalitions in which the two major parties—Catholic and Labor—participated. The two Protestant denominational parties have often joined this coalition and added to its stability. But at the end of 1958 the Labor Party withdrew from the coalition in order to regain independence of action and to forestall possible electoral losses. In the subsequent election (March 1959) Labor indeed held practically its own. But so did the Catholic Party, which again became the strongest single party. The Liberal Party made the most significant gains while the Communists, who immediately after 1945 reached formidable proportions, were reduced to insignificance. There is little likelihood that the Dutch domestic scene will engender much turmoil even if cabinet crises are protracted. Formidable political complications, however, may still be faced in the remaining overseas possessions in the Dutch West Indies and Dutch New Guinea.

Luxembourg, 1945-1959. Luxembourg, too, felt the full weight of German oppression and exploitation in World War II. Of its population, 12% were deported,

[1] The number of those found guilty was in the neighborhood of 50,000—approximately the same number as in Belgium.

and dozens of resistance fighters were shot. A general
strike in 1942 to oppose the draft into the German army
was brutally suppressed. The economy was gravely un-
dermined. Yet the Luxembourgers showed as much
resilience as their neighbors in the other Low Countries.
The principality soon regained its economic and political
equilibrium. Strikes have been virtually unknown since
the war, and major political crises have been equally rare.
As in the other Benelux countries, the Christian-Socialist
(Catholic) and Socialist parties have been dominant since
1945. Elections in February 1959 did not bring about a
major change, although the Liberal Party made sizable
gains (as in the Netherlands). The government remained,
however, in the hands of the Christian-Socialist Party
allied to the Liberals. The only significant change in the
political structure came with the revision of the constitution in 1948. Luxembourg then gave up its traditional
neutrality to side fully with the West. The relations of
the Grand Duchy with its Benelux partners have been
particularly good, and the marriage in 1953 of a Belgian
princess and the Luxembourg heir apparent has further
strengthened common ties.

The Benelux Countries and Foreign Affairs. The
most noteworthy progress and contribution of the Benelux
countries in the postwar world lay in the field of international relations. Belgium, the Netherlands, and Luxembourg are among the states most active in the struggle
for coördination and coöperation within the Western
world. This affirmative attitude has several motivations.
Historically the Low Countries have always supported
peace movements, international conciliation, and collective security. Furthermore, these three countries, which
have the greatest average density of population in Europe,
depend too much on international trade for survival, not
to support peaceful relations among all countries as well
as the drive for enlarged markets. Finally, certain diversi-
ties not to the contrary, the Benelux countries have
enough common interests and features to be the initiators
of the first large-scale attempt at partial integration and
are thus the pacemakers of a new Europe.

In rapid succession the Benelux member states joined
every one of the regional organizations set up to ensure
Europe's revival and survival after World War II. The first

step was the Brussels Pact of 1948, which aligned the Low Countries with Britain and France in a fifty-year alliance designed to guard against a possible attack from a remilitarized Germany. In 1949 the Brussels Pact powers entered NATO. One of the most noteworthy moves toward integration, the project of the Coal and Steel Community in 1950, found the Benelux states among its most ardent supporters. Neither the Council of Europe nor the Western European Union, neither the Common Market nor Euratom, can be thought of without the Benelux countries. Their statesmen, such as the Belgian Paul-Henri Spaak (b. 1899), Joseph Bech (b. 1887) of Luxembourg, and the Dutch foreign ministers Johan Beyen and Joseph Luns have been in the forefront of the struggle for European cooperation and federation.

— 12 —

ECONOMIC STRUCTURE AND UNION OF THE BENELUX COUNTRIES

Above all, Benelux has become a model and a byword for economic integration. Although this integration has taken place only gradually over the last dozen years and encountered many difficulties, the union of the complementary economies of the Low Countries seemed for centuries the most natural of all phases or plans of unification. From the Middle Ages to the end of the nineteenth century each of the three countries developed an economic structure quite different from the other two. Thus Belgium, which had a head start with its linen and cloth industries and early exploitation of its coal resources, became one of the leading manufacturing countries in Europe. The Netherlands, by way of contrast, rose to eminence in commerce, the maritime industries, and dairy and horticultural products. Luxembourg was destined to take a very prominent place, quite out of proportion to the smallness of the country, in the extraction of iron ore and the production of steel. In addition, the Luxembourgers specialized in viniculture and leathermaking.

Thus an unsolicited and unplanned division of labor and raw materials existed for ages. It must be regarded as either a tragic irony or a supreme challenge that when the time for a lasting economic union finally came after 1945 Belgium and the Netherlands had become highly competitive in certain key industries and agricultural sectors, while their fiscal systems and economic policies were further apart than in any other period of history.

Evolution of the Belgian Economy. As has been pointed out, the southern Low Countries had early developed a flourishing textile industry. The Flemish textile industry was the oldest in Europe. Linen manufacture was one of its most important branches. The wool industry had its center in the Liége area (Verviers). Lace was produced in the areas along the French border. Next to the textile industries, a growing metal industry gained importance in the Dinant region (upper Moselle).

Coal was first extracted in the thirteenth century in the Charleroi basin. In the same century Liége developed its famous armaments industry. It also became a center of the evolving glass industry. Thus the southern Low Countries possessed, from the later Middle Ages on, a variegated manufacturing economy which was supported by a flourishing agriculture. The latter was carried on by a peasantry which since the Crusades had become increasingly free from feudal servitude and enjoyed a rising living standard, at least in Flanders and Brabant.

During the Burgundian and Spanish-Habsburg eras, economic progress was curtailed by the centralizing policies of both dynasties. The great religious conflicts of the sixteenth and the extensive wars of the seventeenth century inflicted further setbacks on the once prosperous economy of the southern provinces. Emigration increased and led, among other settlements, to the founding by

Walloon artisans of Neuf-Avesnes (1624), which later became New Amsterdam and then New York. The Austrian rule in the eighteenth century did assist in a partial recovery of the Belgian economy. Imperial protection safeguarded some industrial enterprises, including the new porcelain industry. The introduction of the flying shuttle accelerated output in the linen industry. Attempts to establish great trading companies such as the famous Ostend Company failed owing to the objections of foreign powers, notably the Dutch. Yet Ostend itself prospered and in the 1780's became a serious rival of Amsterdam; whereupon the Dutch closed the Scheldt anew in order to stifle Belgian competition. Only Belgian agriculture made a steady and unchallenged advance in the Austrian era.

The French revolutionary and imperial age had on the whole a beneficial effect on the economy of the southern Low Countries. Especially in Napoleon's time its industrial potential was more fully developed than ever before. The metallurgical industries prospered. Liége became the main producer of arms in Europe. In 1815 the Belgian provinces already had some 90 blast furnaces and 125 iron foundries. The textile industries prospered likewise. Two enterprising industrialists (Lievin Bauwens and William Cockerill) introduced English machinery into the cotton and wool manufacture respectively. Even certain branches of agriculture were industrialized—e.g., the sugarbeet industry, which the French introduced after the British navy cut off their overseas supplies.

Progress in these industries continued into the *Amalgame* period. The latter at first looked very favorable to the interests of Belgian businessmen. A spokesman for this group stated of the union of the Dutch and Belgian peoples: "One eminently commercial and maritime [minded], the other eminently agricultural and manufacturing . . . , reunited under the same sceptre and thus opening . . . to their respective [economies] . . . an equally favorable outlet." From a Belgian point of view this optimism seemed justified. The new king, William I, was in matters economic a progressive and favored the industrial development of his newly acquired southern provinces. The foundation of commercial associations, the establishment of banks, and the availability of credits helped Belgian industry considerably. Above all, the freeing of the Scheldt, the accessibility of Antwerp on an equal footing with the major Dutch ports, and the introduction of a protectionist tariff (1816) stimulated Belgian commerce and manufacture. Antwerp more than doubled the volume of trade cleared through its port between 1818 and 1829. The metal industries boomed and John Cockerill (the son of William) founded at Seraing the largest ironworks in Europe. Among the older industries, linen and coal production rose to new heights. Such industries as crystalmaking (Val St. Lambert) added further to the fame and prosperity of Belgian economy.

With the creation of the Belgian kingdom in 1831 an unavoidable setback took place. The loss of Dutch markets, capital, and governmental support was keenly felt for a while. Moreover, other countries followed a policy of "dumping" as long as Belgium's political and economic situation was not sufficiently stable to enable its government to protect the country. The linen industry, for instance, went into a steep decline which caused widespread unemployment and even famine. Unfortunately, agriculture suffered at the same time from the potato blight in the 1840's and a series of poor harvests.

Not until after mid-century was there a reversal of conditions. Once the liberal Belgian governments were firmly installed, a policy of free trade was followed which greatly benefited a small and rapidly industrialized country that used up only one-fourteenth of its industrial production. As the financial situation improved, more credits became available and further expansion of factories and markets could be undertaken. The cotton industry grew rapidly while the ancient wool industry remained prosperous. The linen industry, however, declined further, owing to cheap foreign competition. But the light and heavy metal industries flourished, as did armaments and rolling stock production, and Belgium was one of the leading industrial countries on the European continent. The early creation of a railroad system greatly assisted in this development. By 1875 Belgium possessed a complete network, which remained one of the densest in the world. The production of coal was further stepped up, but lignite, anthracite, and coke had to be imported. New industries were created, and of these the chemical industry assumed major proportions. By 1914 nearly 45% of the population were engaged in industry.

In agriculture, too, considerable progress was made. The small family holding formed the backbone of Belgian farming. Flanders produced the largest amount of wheat. In Brabant and the Hesbaye, horse breeding led to the large-scale export of the famous Belgian draft horses. Hog raising constituted the second most important branch of livestock development. Unlike many industrial groups and sectors, the Belgian farmer sought support from protective tariffs, introduced by the Catholic Party governments beginning in the 1880's. Such organizations as the powerful Boerenbond served as a means of self-protection and self-advancement for the Belgian peasantry. But in spite of support and protection it was as yet unable to provide adequately for the nutritional needs of the country.

During World War I the Belgian economy suffered grievously from German occupation.[1] In the postwar years rehabilitation was therefore the primary concern. Within half a dozen years most of the damages were repaired. But just when Belgium seemed well on the road to full recovery, a severe financial crisis set in. In anticipation of German reparations, which were unexpectedly slow in coming, the authorities had spent excessively. Gold coverage had become very thin and the currency plummeted in a deep inflationary spiral. In 1926 a ministry of national concentration pegged the currency at about one-seventh of its former value. For a few years Belgium, like so many other European countries, pulled ahead only to be hit the harder by the Great Depression. Exports fell rapidly and by 1932 some 25% of the industrial labor force was unemployed. Recovery was gradually brought about, especially by the bold measures of Paul van Zeeland (b. 1893) who formed his first cabinet in 1935. The rate of interest was lowered and credit cheapened. The currency was again devalued, but Belgium remained the last European country with a gold standard.

[1] See pp. 77-78.

Apart from these great crises, many Belgian industries curtailed their production during the inter-bellum period or became stationary. The growth rate of Belgian industry fell far behind that of most Western countries. Thus the glass industry, which before 1900 held practically a world monopoly for plate glass and bottles, was reduced to one-fourth of the world production. Coal production became inadequate even for domestic needs, notwithstanding the tapping of large new fields in the Campine region. Textile manufacture ran into heavy competition from such cheaper producers as Japan and India. On the other hand, the chemical industries were expanded and electrification of the country was greatly advanced. But probably the most important single event in the structure of Belgian economy was the economic union with Luxembourg, concluded in 1921.

The Economy of Luxembourg and the Creation of the Belgium Luxembourg Economic Union (B.L.E.U.). Luxembourg's economy was of necessity far less stratified than the economies of the other Low Countries. Its traditional mainstays were agriculture and iron ore mining. The latter led to the establishment of foundries in the fourteenth century. But the iron industry remained the only one of importance to the eve of the French Revolution. Tanneries became the second largest industry, while the manufacture of paper, china, and draperies had modest beginnings. Viniculture and the sugarbeet industry were foremost in the agrarian sector. Unfortunately, the potential of the Luxembourg economy was disregarded in the *Amalgame* era. Not until the 1840's did a decisive change occur.

In 1842 the grand duchy joined the German customs union. The Luxembourgers preferred a customs union with France, as they did again in 1921, but power politics prevented this solution. Yet Luxembourg needed to fuse its economy with that of a larger country in order to exist. On the whole, membership in the Zollverein benefited the principality, which utilized the large German markets for its iron, leather, paper, and wine products. Two specific events greatly assisted the growth of Luxembourg's economy. The first railroad was constructed in 1859. It was so significant an episode that a poem, the *Feierwôn,* written for this occasion, became the national anthem. Some twenty years later the Thomas-Gilchrist process of steel manufacturing revolutionized the iron industry, so that production jumped in a single decade from 25,000 to 250,000 tons. The high-phosphorus iron ore, the famous *minette*, could now be fully utilized. Progress in agriculture was somewhat slower, but scientific methods gradually prevailed and the yield was increased. By 1914 Luxembourg's economy provided a comfortable living for nearly all of its citizens.

The deprivations of World War I were felt all the more by the Luxembourgers. After 1918 they got rid of the Germans for good, but were then faced with the problem of entering into a new economic partnership. France was generally regarded as the most desirable senior partner. But the French government had already officially disinterested itself in 1917 in order to boost Belgian morale. The Belgians were eager to restore at least partly the union of 1831, but the Luxembourgers showed less readiness to accept a union which was confined to the economies of the two countries. Agrarian interests, especially, felt safer behind the protective French tariff wall. Yet in spite of considerable opposition, including that of industrial sectors which feared the smallness of the domestic Belgian market and possible discrimination in transportation costs, the economic union was voted into existence in 1921. The new union proved more advantageous and stable than had been predicted. Minor differences remained, but the proven viability of B.L.E.U. inspired the creators of the larger Benelux economic system.

The Evolution of the Dutch Economy.   The third partner in Benelux followed for centuries a very different economic development from the B.L.E.U. member states. Since the Middle Ages the Dutch had developed an economy which was primarily commercial and agricultural. A small textile industry had come into being in the thirteenth century but could not compete with the quality and quantity of the output of Flanders and Brabant. Not until the nineteenth century did a sizable cotton industry develop in Overijssel, which eventually could compete with Belgian production. In almost all other branches of industry such competition was avoided until the twentieth century. The exceptions were the paper and diamond industries. The former did not gain much prominence in either country, but the latter caused considerable rivalry. Diamond cutting and polishing flourished first in Bruges; then the industry moved to Amsterdam as the result of the great religious schism. Later still, Antwerp rivaled Amsterdam, while most recently the diamond industry has moved back to Belgium.

The Dutch were free from such challenges in most other sectors of their economy. Foremost among these were shipbuilding and fisheries on the one hand and dairy production and horticulture on the other. The products of Dutch shipwrights were in demand everywhere, including the American colonies. Dutch ships alone reputedly numbered more than 20,000 of all types, with crews totaling nearly a quarter of a million men by mid-seventeenth century. A decline in the following centuries was largely caused by the lack of naval stores. But in the twentieth century a noteworthy recovery took place. Today many foreign countries rely again on Dutch shipyards, and the Dutch merchant marine ranks seventh in the world. Of similar importance for a long time was the fishing industry. The herring fishery has been traditionally one of the most essential branches of Dutch economy, ever since the introduction in 1384 of salting for preservation. The Dutch also engaged in whaling expeditions and still do so today.

Next to the maritime industries, dairy production formed the mainstay of the economic structure of the Netherlands. Since the end of the Middle Ages an increasing amount of produce has been exported. Foremost were the famed cheeses of Alkmaar, Edam, and Gouda. From the Leiden area, butter was sent to all parts of the world. The main regions of dairy production were Friesland and Holland. They became famous for their cows, which produced an extraordinary amount of milk. Wheat was grown mainly in Zeeland and Groningen province. Horticulture was another important branch of agricultural production. The tulips grown near Haarlem gained world renown. Tobacco growing became likewise of considerable importance. All these activities were made possible by a peasantry which since medieval times had gained steadily in freedom, self-reliance, ability, and prosperity. The coöperatives formed since the end of the nineteenth century constitute a striking expression of this progress. Before World War II dairy and horticultural exports accounted for one-third of the value of all imports, and this ratio increased to 40% in postwar years. Other food industries have likewise greatly expanded. The Netherlands is now the world's largest beer producer. Its chocolate, margarine, and canned-food industries are very substantial.

The third major sector of the Dutch economy is commerce. Foreign trade became a necessity for a country whose ports in some cases numbered more ships than houses. Many of the old Dutch cities had been members of the Hanseatic League. By the sixteenth century the traders of Holland and Zeeland were the most active in Europe and ranged from the Mediterranean to the Baltic. The following century saw the penetration by Dutch seamen and merchants of the four corners of the globe and the rise of Amsterdam as the foremost trading and banking center of Europe. Although neither the Netherlands nor its capital city could maintain this leading position, neither ever fell afterward to a negligible rank in world trade. In the last hundred years a strong revival has taken place. Thanks to the mechanization of transportation (including the excellent road-rail-and-canal systems), the consistent free-trade policies, and the needs of such new and large neighboring countries as Germany, the Netherlands resumed its leading role in international commerce. Rotterdam is today the second largest port in the world and as *Europort* (into which it will be expanded) will serve the whole of Western Europe. As far as the ratio of trade to the size of population is concerned, the Netherlands outranks all other countries in the world.

To the main branches of Dutch economy, outlined above, there has been added a steadily growing industry. Since the 1870's the Netherlands has been developing its industrial potential and tapping its meager domestic resources for this purpose. Coal mining was undertaken and some iron ore extracted in Limburg province. The Royal Dutch Petroleum Company, later merged with the Shell Company, built an increasing number of refineries. At the end of World War I a steel mill was erected near IJmuiden, and others have been constructed since. A major industry developed at Eindhoven, where the Philips works produced a great variety of electrical equipment. This plant has become the largest in the Netherlands, with over 30,000 workers today. Another important industry to expand rapidly was that of rayon and artificial silk. The chemical industries expanded likewise in the inter-bellum period. Thus the Netherlands had embarked on an ambitious program of industrialization before World War II. The abundance of raw materials in the East Indies greatly helped in this development and at the same time furnished many opportunities for Dutch investments.

World War II put a temporary stop to the further industrial growth of the Netherlands, and the German occupation reduced the economy to substandard levels. It was this unfortunate situation which faced the proponents of the Benelux economic union after 1945. The difference between the Belgian and Dutch economies had become such that the gap appeared at times too wide to be bridged. Moreover, certain sectors in both economies had become highly competitive instead of remaining complementary. Finally, there was the residue of traditional economic rivalries and the remembrance of past conflicts.

The Benelux Venture. In spite of these handicaps, representatives of the three Benelux governments in exile drew up a bold plan of economic integration under the agreement of September 1944. (*See Reading No. 20.*) They disregarded in a praiseworthy move such historic causes of tension as the control or expansion of inland waterways and fears of commercial competition. The fundamental hindrances standing in the way of the envisaged economic integration were of more recent vintage and more difficult to overcome. Hopes had run high immediately after World War II that Europe's first regional association would also be the first one to succeed. But events seemed to prove differently. So far from starting on terms of equality, as had been envisaged in 1944, the economies of Belgium and the Netherlands were separated by a wide margin. Dutch war losses were estimated at over 30% of the prewar national wealth as against between 6% and 8% for Belgium.

The latter country had preserved intact the wealth of the Congo region—now the center of Belgium's No. 1 problem. The Belgian government introduced in 1945 an effective currency reform, which stopped inflation as well as the black market. Dollar and gold reserves were rapidly increased, and Belgium became in fact the only European country with a reversed lend-lease claim vis à vis the United States. Belgium's partner Luxembourg underwent a similar quick recovery from the ravages of the war. The steel industry made a striking comeback. Although Luxembourg is one of the smallest countries in the world, it ranks eleventh in steel production; within Benelux it produces about 31% of the steel output. Other branches of the economy recovered in like manner. Luxembourg has become one of the countries with the highest wage levels, and in per capita wealth leads all Europe except Switzerland.

In contradistinction to the B.L.E.U. countries, the Netherlands in the immediate postwar period was one of the poorest countries in Europe. The Nazis had dealt with this once so prosperous land like locusts. Food supplies had either been carried off or destroyed by flooding. Industrial plants had either been stripped or ruined and production had fallen off as much as 75% in certain industries. Two factors further complicated the situation of the Dutch at the end of the war. Population growth reached extraordinary proportions after 1945 in contrast to Belgium, whose demographic curve is the lowest in Western Europe. The Netherlands has become the most densely populated country in the world with over 877 people per square mile as against 760 in Belgium and 312 in Luxembourg. There are now over eleven million Dutch (compared with nine million Belgians and 312,000 Luxembourgers) in an area which has somewhat increased by reclamation but is insufficient for the maintenance of a rapidly growing population. Emigration has become very marked in the postwar period and now involves about 50,000 people annually.

The other reason for the Dutch spiral descent to economic rock bottom was the extent to which the Germans ruthlessly exploited the country at a time when they had already withdrawn from the other Low Countries. Moreover, the Dutch had met with Teutonic thoroughness most of the German requisitions, while Belgians and Luxembourgers had utilized every subterfuge to forestall payments and deliveries of goods. To add to the grievous losses thus sustained, the Netherlands lost

the largest ·and most flourishing part of its once so
formidable colonial empire when Indonesia, after prolonged and bitter conflict, attained independence in 1949.
In spite of these handicaps, the Dutch achieved a most
remarkable economic upturn. Austerity, determination,
industriousness, civic spirit, and careful planning alike
made this recovery possible.

Trials and Tribulations of Benelux. In order to
accomplish their goals, successive Dutch governments
had recourse to rigid planning, low wages and prices, extensive subsidies, and a "soft" currency. Belgium and
Luxembourg, on the other hand, followed consistently
a policy of high wages and prices, free enterprise, and a
"hard" currency with restricted subsidies and credits.
Before the war Dutch wages were about one-third higher
than those of the B.L.E.U. But this situation was completely reversed after 1945. There was also a wide difference in rents, which were much lower and strictly
controlled in the Netherlands. Moreover, the fiscal and
social security systems differed widely. Thus, for instance,
transmission (sales) taxes were much higher in Belgium
than in the Netherlands, while conversely the sugar duties
in the latter country were eleven times as high as in
Belgium. Again, in the early 1950's Belgians and Luxembourgers paid between one-half and two-thirds more
for social benefits than did the Dutch.

Notwithstanding these divergences, a gradual alignment
was effected on a number of issues. As the monetary
situation of the Netherlands improved, its currency
hardened and its foreign exchange reserves increased.
Wages were slowly increased and the discrepancy with
B.L.E.U. wages partly overcome. Excise duties on most
products were adjusted in the three Benelux states. A
tariff community was established in 1948, which quickly
assumed the character of a customs union. But the
anticipated economic union in which movements of goods,
persons, and capital were to be entirely free had to be
postponed again and again.

Just when such union seemed possible by 1952 due to
the greatly improved position of the Netherlands, now
an equal of B.L.E.U., new difficulties arose. Hitherto
the agricultural sectors of Benelux had been most sensitive
to the over-all policy of trade liberalization which char-

acterized the second phase of evolution of the projected economic union. Dutch agriculture, based on farm holdings somewhat larger than those in Belgium (an average of 22 against 17 acres and roughly 30 acres in Luxembourg), could produce much more cheaply and on a larger scale than its heavily protected Belgian counterpart. Competition was especially keen in horticultural products. In order to mollify B.L.E.U. interests, largely geared to cover domestic needs, an agreement between the Benelux partners was worked out in 1950 which provided for special regulations concerning specific produce.

The main area of direct conflict then shifted to certain branches of industry. The Dutch, who had started in many cases from scratch, built up-to-date plants which often outproduced the older and sometimes antiquated Belgian industries.[1] When the Dutch began to export to the B.L.E.U. on a large scale, the cry of "Dumping!" went up among Belgian producers. Objections were raised especially in the furniture, paper, tobacco, textile, and footwear industries. In 1953 the whole Benelux system seemed on the verge of a breakup. But to the lasting credit of the populations and governments of the Benelux countries, a final showdown was averted. The trials and tribulations in the end strengthened the determination to find a way toward union.

In 1954 an agreement was reached on the free movement of capital, and two years later a similar treaty provided for the free movement of labor. The main objectives of the planned economic union were at last in sight. Substantial progress was made toward further trade liberalization, which is now 97% free in industrial goods (but much lower for agricultural products). Most important, the Benelux countries have now been recognized as a single trading unit and have been represented at international meetings by a common spokesman. The much-heralded and often postponed economic union

---

[1] Difficulties of this nature are not restricted to the relations of Belgium and the Netherlands. Within the larger framework of the European Coal and Steel Community, Belgian mines are at present working at a loss (subsidized by the other five member states) since many of them are unprofitable. The closing of such mines has led most recently to disturbances in the Borinage.

was finally written into the Treaty of February 3, 1958.
It will go into effect as soon as it is ratified. A near-com-
plete voluntary union of the Benelux countries is thus
likely to be attained within a decade.

— 13 —

CONCLUSION

The age-old question, whether the Low Countries are
a historic, cultural, geographic, and economic unit
artifically kept apart throughout much of their history, or
are different entities that could at most be brought together
into a temporary union for brief periods by external
force or autocratic measures, is about to be answered.
The Benelux states have entered into a closer union
than ever before in history. Bitter necessity and experience
alike have made such union possible. Today Belgium,
the Netherlands, and Luxembourg have at least partially
achieved an integration which Charlemagne, the Burgundian dukes, William the Silent, Charles V, Philip II
of Spain, Napoleon I, and King William I attempted in
vain to bring about. Beyond economic fusion an identity
of views, a community of interests, and a similarity of
institutions have been established.

The process of molding the Low Countries into a whole,
however incomplete as yet, has been facilitated by certain
developments. In the age of blocs and superpowers it is
evident that there can be no survival for smaller countries
without some measure of federation. What could be more
rational and natural than a tight association of three
countries in many ways so close to each other? In
domestic affairs, too, similarities are now far more in
evidence than dissimilarities. The traditional differences of
a political, economic, and cultural nature have either

diminished or disappeared. Political structure and atti-
tudes have become very much alike. In matters economic
the Netherlands is now almost as industrialized as its
partners. If a division of labor can be brought about, the
industrial sectors will ultimately become complementary
rather than competitive. In religion, too, the great divide
has been partly overcome. The Catholic population in the
North now constitutes nearly 40% of the Dutch population and is a force equal to that of the Protestant groups.
Catholicism is in fact a major influence in the further
integration of the Benelux countries.

But the most significant of the changes wrought is the
dynamic transition of concepts from the vague geographic
term Low Countries to the much more meaningful expression Benelux, connoting a deliberate process toward
creation of a supranational unit by voluntary association
and popular consent. Benelux, it must be remembered,
is a three-syllable composite and betokens a threefold
unity of purpose and equality of participation by all three
constituent partners. The great wheel of history has come
full circle and the three countries now form an entirety as
they did in an incomparably more primitive and uncon-
scious form two thousand years ago.

It should be kept in mind, however, that this process of
integration does not entail or even foresee the establishment of a single and uniform state. There will be no
common sovereign, no common parliament, no common
law code, no common currency. All indications point to
the likelihood that the Benelux countries will seek, as
truly democratic states, a pluralistic system of federation. Their peoples look for union through diversity rather
than for oneness through uniformity. After two millennia
the inhabitants of Belgium, the Netherlands, the Luxembourg have learned, among many other things, the significance of the motto in the coat of arms of one of them:
UNION MAKES STRENGTH.

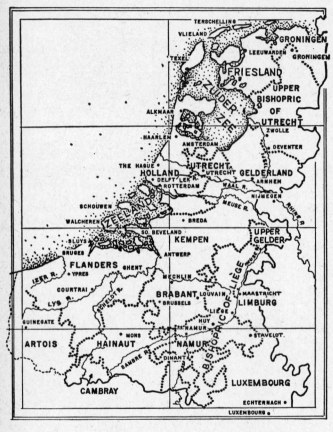

THE LOW COUNTRIES AT THE END OF THE MIDDLE AGES.

Part II

READINGS

BISHOP THEODUIN OF LIÉGE GRANTS A CHARTER TO THE CITY OF HUY, 1066[1]

This charter is one of the oldest extant in Europe. While it is not very elaborate, it may be considered a model for similar though much more extensive grants in the following centuries. It is not just by fortuitous circumstance that one of the first city charters was granted to a city in the Low Countries, the region with the relatively largest concentration of urban centers in Western Europe.

✓   ✓   ✓

I, Theoduin, by the Grace of God Bishop of Liége, wish it to be known to the present as well as to future generations, how, after the grant of freedom to the church of Huy, first given through consecration by the lord Bishop Maternus of blessed memory, I have granted freedom also to the city.

I have rebuilt the aforementioned church. . . . I have also enriched the church. . . . The aforenamed city has given me, in exchange for its freedom, first of all, one-third of all its movable property to defray the necessary expenses for the church; in order to enjoy this freedom on a larger scale, it has afterwards given half its movable property.

The first freedom is this, that after the peaceful death of the bishop until the full installation of another the burghers of the city shall maintain in good faith and with

* The translation is by Professor Ernest McDonnell.
[1] Georg Waitz, ed., *Urkunden zur deutschen Verfassungsgeschichte,* 2d edn. (Berlin, 1886), pp. 9-11.

sound policy the castle of Huy from the income of the city. . . .

But if we or one of our successors should try to infringe upon the freedom granted above or upon any of their rights not mentioned herein, we have granted and determined that the Duke of Lorraine and others, both clergy and laity hereafter named, shall not neglect to come to their aid effectively in order to preserve their freedom and rights, but only after a warning has first been sent. . . .

Done in the year after the incarnation of Our Lord 1066, in the 4th indiction, in the 18th year of our pontificate, and in the 11th year of the reign of Henry.

— Reading No. 2 —

THE CHARTER OF LUXEMBOURG CITY, AUGUST, 1244 [2]

The progress of municipal liberties can be readily gauged if the Charter of Luxembourg City is compared with that of Huy, nearly two hundred years earlier. By mid-thirteenth century the burgher class in the Low Countries already constituted a political power.

✓   ✓   ✓

In the name of the Holy and Indivisible Trinity. Ermesendis, Countess of Luxembourg, to all her subjects forever. We wish it to be known to all the faithful of Christ both present and future that, anxious to secure the peace and tranquillity of our burgesses in Luxem-

[2] Fr.-X. Würth-Paquet and N. van Werveke, *Cartulaire ou recueil des documents politiques et administratif de la ville de Luxembourg* (Luxembourg, 1881), pp. 5-9.

bourg, we have decreed that the same be honored with
the privilege of liberty, declaring in the following the
liberty granted to the same together with the rights and
services to be rendered in the future to us and our successors, Counts or Countesses of Luxembourg in the event
there shall be no count.

The scabini [aldermen] and burgesses shall elect the
justicarius [mayor], who is to be of the said liberty, with
the same to be presented to the lord of the place and by
him set in office. He must, after taking the oath, protect
the rights of the Count or Countess as well as the rights
of the burgesses and their liberties. He will remain in his
office for only a year, unless the lord of the place, the
aldermen, and burgesses mutually agree that he should
remain longer.

The aldermen are to be appointed in accordance with
the form hitherto observed; they are to protect the
rights of the Lord or Lady and of the advocate of
Luxembourg, as well as the rights of the burgesses. They
shall also seek and find advice concerning the carrying
out of judgments and consultations of law, where and
in like manner as they have been up to now accustomed to
seek and find them.

The said burgesses by common consent have agreed
to this, that to us and our successors, Lords of Luxembourg, each burgess shall give every year forever fourteen
Luxembourg denars. . . .

Whosoever of the burgesses of the liberty of Luxembourg shall wish to sell grain inside of Luxembourg or
the region of its jurisdiction, shall sell it to the measure
of the Count or Countess; and the burgess of Luxembourg
buying shall pay to the Count or Countess a fiftieth part
of this grain which he buys; and if in a sale which he has
made secretly he shall not have paid the excise . . . ,
he shall pay the same excise notwithstanding and five
shillings as fine. In the case of grain purchased, the
shillings shall not be paid but only the aforementioned
excise.

The burgesses of Luxembourg, when a notice of eight
days has been sent out, shall go on military expedition
of the Lord or Lady of Luxembourg, providing for themselves out of their own means for the first eight days.

. . . And after eight days have passed, for as long as they shall be on the said expedition, the Lord or Lady of Luxembourg will furnish them in everything. A burgess who at the summons of the towncrier shall not have gone on the expedition . . . shall pay as fine ten shillings if he is a mounted soldier, and five shillings if a foot soldier, unless he shall have been prevented by a legitimate excuse.

Each burgess who is able to have a horse and armor shall have these . . . and he who is not able to have a horse and armor shall have a doublet, lance, and helmet, according to the decision of the mayor and aldermen; and if having to have a horse and armor on the day announced to him he shall not have these, he shall pay ten shillings as fine, and a foot soldier five shillings if on a day similarly announced to him he shall not have the above-mentioned armor; however after the following fortnight they must have the horses and armor according to the aforementioned manner, and if they omit to do this, when the fortnight has elapsed, a mounted soldier shall pay ten shillings and a foot soldier five shillings as fine, to be multiplied from fortnight to fortnight for as long as they omit to secure the horses and armor.

The burgesses shall give to their Count two hundred Luxembourg pounds when he becomes a knight, and to the Countess, if there is no male count, as many pounds when she marries for the first time and if she marries for a second time they will give her nothing. If the Count of the oftnamed place has several sons who will become knights, the two hundred pounds shall be given only to the first-born when he becomes a knight, and likewise if there is no son, to the eldest daughter when she marries for the first time.

The burgesses mentioned shall have the same use in the waters, pastures, and woods of the Lord or Lady Luxembourg, which they had up to now. . . . No burgess is to hunt with dogs, nets, sacks or other instrument whatsoever, and he will pay five shillings as fine if he should be caught hunting while doing any of the aforementioned. They may, however, fowl there with hawks or other birds.

Item, the Count or Countess of Luxembourg can of their own accord choose four or more of the freedom of the town, with the advice however of the mayor, aldermen, and burgesses, to collect the excise coming from sales and the fines, which will have to be paid . . . and those who shall have been deputed to the said office shall have six denars jointly from each fine; they are to be removed by the Count or Countess if all or any of the same shall be lacking [in duty], with the advice, however, of the mayor, aldermen and burgesses.

No one shall remain in Luxembourg [City], within the walls or without, unless he be a burgess and of the liberty of Luxembourg, with the exception of soldiers and others who are expressly excepted from the Charter. . . .

The burgesses of Luxembourg as regards their persons and possessions shall enjoy liberty and security forever, except for those things which are written above and with the exception of the fines which on account of the transgressions of the people have been customarily paid in accordance with the decision of the aldermen.

To the observance therefore of the above and especially of the liberty granted to the oftnamed burgesses, we have bound ourselves by this corporeal oath; also our sons Henry and Gerard have sworn the same. . . . Also to their heirs, when they ask for their fee, the same shall not be granted by us or our successors, Lords of Luxembourg, unless they first take the oath which the person whom they succeed shall have taken; to the observance of which we have also bound ourselves by oath. And whatsoever things we have sworn, . . . our successors shall be held to swear; against the same [oath], we will not knowingly attempt anything, neither we or our successors. But if through ignorance something of the above shall not have been observed, we will be held to make amends for it, and likewise our successors, within forty days, if so requested by the burgesses. In order, moreover, that it may have the force of perpetual strength, we have affixed to the present writing our seal and have had affixed the seals of our faithful men named. We also, Henry and Gerard, sons of the above-mentioned Countess, have added our seals to the said writing, approving the things which are above written and testifying that we have sworn to observe the same. Dated at Luxembourg, in the year of our Lord twelve hundred and forty four, in the month of August.

— Reading No. 3* —

JOHN II GRANTS FINANCIAL AND JUDICIAL PRIVILEGES TO BRABANT AND ESTABLISHES THE COUNCIL OF CORTENBERG, SEPTEMBER 27, 1312³

This noteworthy grant of liberties and governmental codetermination on the part of the Brabant citizenry was the first major regional charter in the Low Countries. It vouchsafed a degree of self-government and served as a model for later charters, which gradually established the rights of the citizens to partake in government and to enjoy a measure of constitutional guarantees.

✦   ✦   ✦

In the name of the Father, the Son, and the Holy Spirit whose invocation is a good beginning and the best ending. We John, by the grace of God Duke of Lotharingia, Brabant, and Limburg, leaving all malice behind, and especially because of the constancy and the faithful service which the people of our lands have always rendered to our forefathers and us, and which we hope they shall continue to render in the future, have granted our people and lands in common, with full realization, with deliberation and full, mature counsel, and with common and full execution, and demand that all the

---

* The translation is by Professor McDonnell.
³ Jos. van der Straeten, *Het charter en de raad van Kortenberg* in *Université de Louvain, Recueil de travaux d'histoire et de philologie, 3me Série, Fascicule 47* (Louvain, Brussels, 1952), pp. 12-19.

points and articles, which are stipulated hereafter, shall be maintained and observed forever.

1. In the first place we, our heirs, and our successors shall never take lodging or seize beds in our lands except for knighthood, marriage, or imprisonment and then the beds shall be appropriated in such a way that none of our people will be molested or injured.

2. We further subject our lands to law and justice, and our people, rich and poor, shall pass law and judgment just as the letters, composed for the purpose, recommend and in such a way that the said letters on judgments shall be endowed with good sound advice; if any point is to be amended or is too severe in any respect for our people and lands, it shall always be amended and alleviated with the advice of the good people of our land and with those who shall be chosen or appointed for that purpose, just as is stipulated hereafter.

3. Furthermore our heirs and successors shall maintain our free cities in their liberties and rights which they have inherited, and shall maintain and treat the good people of the cities according to the law of each city, in all matters. . . .

4. Furthermore we and our successors shall, at the common advice of our lands, chose from the lands four knights, the best qualified and best educated who can be found, for the good of the country; and three good men of Louvain, three good burghers of Brussels, one good man of Antwerp, one from Bois-le-Duc, one from Tirlemont, and one from Leuwe.

5. And these who have been thus selected shall assemble at Cortenberg [the ducal residence half-way between Brussels and Louvain] every three weeks and shall be empowered (which power we have given them for us and our successors) to hear and to judge if there is any violation of the points stipulated above in the lands in any matter, or shall occur hereafter, in whatever manner. . . .

6. They shall have full power in our behalf and on the part of our successors to provide for and amend all these matters. . . .

7. Furthermore, if it should happen that any of the aforesaid, our knights, or the other good people who have been selected for this purpose dies or does not act for

the common good, then another shall be chosen and installed in his place at Cortenberg, at the advice of the others and the burghers of the land.

8. And these knights and good people who are chosen for this purpose shall swear by the Saints and on the Holy Gospels that they shall defend us and our successors and all the people of our lands, rich and poor, according to their power and maintain each in his rights and administer justice according to their best ability.

9. And should it happen that the aforesaid knights and burghers at Cortenberg make, project, or ordain any matters, or we or our successors or anyone else violate or fail to maintain these matters, we agree and will for ourselves and our successors that no judgment shall be handed down in our land, no service shall be rendered, until it is ascertained that the business has been conducted as has been prescribed.

10. And all these aforesaid matters, point by point, as have been prescribed above, we promise faithfully and swear by the Saints and on the Holy Gospels, for ourselves, our heirs, and successors, for the benefit and advantage of ourselves and our land and all our people to maintain and cause to be maintained forever fast and firm without opposition from us, our heirs, or successors, or anyone else, and we promise that we or our successors or any of our partisans shall never resort to subtlety, intrigue, or subterfuge or inflict penalties by which we could undermine these matters in any way.

11. And for the greater security and everlasting support of these matters we bid, order, and exhort all our barons, knights, both bannerets and others, and all whoever they may be who possess or hold fiefs in our lands, as well as the burghers of our cities, great and small, and the men who owe us homage and fealty, that they promise to maintain all the aforesaid matters, point by point as they promised above, and all other matters which we have arranged for this purpose, for them and their successors, forever, fast and firm.

12. We further bid, order, and command all the aforesaid who are now or shall be in the future in the aforesaid homage and fealty—should it happen that we, our heirs, or successors oppose the aforementioned matters and points in whole or part, or violate them in any

manner—that they shall not perform homage to us, our heirs, or successors, and shall not be subject until such time as we have corrected or caused to be remedied all the infractions that have occurred, in the forms as have been prescribed and stipulated above.

13. And should it happen that any of our barons, knights, bannerets, or others, or anyone else who holds fee under us, or people of our cities who are now or will be subject to us in the future, wish to violate any of the aforesaid points or oppose them in any way, or who intend to oppose them, we consider them before us, our heirs, and successors, criminal and disloyal, no longer able to enjoy any decision, law, or judgment.

14. We further bid . . . and admonish all . . . in the aforesaid homage and fealty that they shall forever maintain all the aforesaid matters . . . and support them with energy and might if they should be endangered in any way.

15. . . . In acknowledgment, confirmation and eternal recognition of all these matters which are prescribed above we, John, by the grace of God Duke, seal with our seal these present letters, and bid amicably and earnestly our beloved faithful [here follow the names] . . . our beloved people of our cities and of our market-places . . . that they hang their seals with care on these present letters in recognition of truth and in constancy and eternal confirmation of all the aforementioned matters and points. . . . These letters were made in the year of the Incarnation of Our Lord as one writes MCCC and twelve, in the month of September on Wednesday before Saint Bavon.

THE JOYEUSE ENTRÉE OF THE DUKE AND DUCHESS OF BRABANT, JANUARY 3, 1356 [4]

The Joyeuse Entrée (Joyous Entry) must be regarded as the Magna Charta of the southern Low Countries. But unlike the famed English document, the Joyeuse Entrée reflects the demands and interests of the citizenry in the large and numerous cities of Brabant rather than of feudal nobility. That constitutional claims of Belgian citizens should for centuries be based on this fundamental charter attests to its significance.

✦   ✦   ✦

Jeanne, by the grace of God Duchess of Luxembourg, Lotharingia, Brabant, and Limburg, and Marchioness of the Holy Empire; and Wenceslas of Bohemia, by the grace of God Duke of the same lands and margrave of the Holy Empire, as her lawful husband and protector, make known to all who shall see these letters or hear them read. . . .

I. First we promise the good people of our aforesaid cities and land to endow our sisters, as our cities and lands shall ordain, without dividing the country.

II. We further promise and agree that the privileges and charters which pertain to our beloved lord and father, the Duke of Brabant (may God keep his soul!), us, our good people and lands, and which are now located at Louvain, or which we and our good land shall henceforth obtain, shall always be under the protection and in the

---

* The translation is by Professor McDonnell.
[4] Ria van Bragt, *De Blijde Inkomst van de Hertogen van Brabant Johanna en Wenceslas* in *Anciens pays et Assemblées d'Etats*, XIII (Louvain, 1956), pp. 95-109.

safekeeping of our cities of Brabant, for our own good and that of our commonwealth; and they shall never be removed or alienated without the will and consent of our good cities of Brabant. There shall be three keys to them; one of which we shall possess, our city of Louvain shall have the second, and our city of Brussels the third, so that one shall never work without the others. We shall keep copies of these privileges and charters, and our common cities shall do likewise, for the good of our aforesaid commonwealth and to help us and them in the counsel of our cities.

III. We further promise that we shall never hereafter form an alliance without the will and consent of our cities and our commonwealth, or have any matters sealed with our great seal whereby our lands and the boundaries of Brabant—insofar as they belonged to our aforesaid lord and father on whichever side of the Meuse—shall in any way be diminished or contracted. This seal shall be deposited in Brussels, and there shall be three keys for it just as is the case for the privileges located at Louvain.

IV. We further promise that henceforth we shall admit no one to our sworn council unless he is a citizen of Brabant. . . .

V. We further promise that it will be possible to travel peacefully and to pass through whatsoever region with the payment of customary tolls, . . .

VI. We further promise to keep our public roads open and free insofar as we are obligated to so, without deceit, each person being at liberty to travel at the customary toll, except for debts or obligations which he has incurred or contracted, or for crimes or misdeeds which he may have committed.

VII. We further promise to keep the aforesaid lands intact and undivided without mortgage, sale, alienation, or encumbrance in any way; and that we, Duke Wencelas, shall transmit the aforesaid lands after the death of our beloved spouse, Duchess Jeanne, undivided and undiminished to the legitimate heirs of Brabant who are obligated to remain, and also that the aforesaid lands shall henceforth remain undivided and undiminished from heir to heir, the rightful heir being obligated to remain. . . .

VIII. We promise further to maintain and strengthen the peace of the land as it has been made and ordained.

IX. We, the Duke and Duchess, further promise to maintain and strengthen the bonds which have been made between us, our good people and the land of Brabant, and the Count of Flanders, his good people and lands, just as the letters indicate which have been drafted for this purpose and sealed; and similarly, to maintain the bond between us, our good people, and Brabant and the good people and bishopric of Liége.

X. We further promise that we shall never declare war or cause plunder or allow such action except at the advice, will, and consent of our good cities and lands, unless war or attack is made on us first. . . .

XI. We further promise that whenever we grant anyone in the future a mayoralty (*meyerie*) or forestry (*voirsterye*) or create a mayoralty or forestry the mayor (*meyer*) or forester (*voirster*) shall not farm out or grant the mayorship or forestry to another person, but shall keep it and discharge his duties.

XII. We further promise that anyone arrested in Brabant shall not be transferred outside Brabant.

XIII. We further promise that not a penny shall be struck except with the advice of our commonwealth and that the penny shall never be debased without its consent. . . .

XIV. We further promise that no one who is not of legitimate birth shall be counsellor, magistrate, or judge in Brabant or hold any office in our behalf; and that magistrates . . . shall be removed and changed annually.

XV. We further promise that an investigation shall be conducted annually in behalf of our country, to wit, that all judges and all those with the powers to do right or wrong in Brabant in our behalf shall give account henceforth annually. . . .

XVI. We further promise that in the event some dispute or controversy arises in these lands all those who are innocent of the dispute or controversy shall enjoy firm and solid peace from the time the dispute or controversy begins until noon of the following day, and if anyone commits an act in the meantime, we shall declare him a breaker of the peace.

XVII. We further promise that we shall grant land to no murderer unless he becomes reconciled with the relatives [of the victim].

XVIII. We further promise that if a citizen of our lands of Brabant, Huesden, and the region beyond the Meuse has, with deliberation and premeditation, incited anyone outside these borders to revolt or presumed to do so, he has forfeited his life and goods as if he had committed murder; nor shall we ever return the property to him. If it happens that he returns to our country, we shall bring him to justice like a criminal. Similarly, whoever of our aforesaid lands commits another act abroad shall be guilty like the others.

XIX. We further grant that no one in our lands can summon a fellow citizen from outside this land for any reason except for testamentary cases, marriage contracts, or alms; who acts otherwise shall incur penalty of life and goods, and we shall never restore him in our land.

XX. We further promise that those who are banned from our lands for insurrection, murder, theft, or rape shall remain banned forever, and shall never again be allowed to reënter our lands.

XXI. We further consent and agree that if a woman or girl is violated against her will and she wishes to live with the man, she shall commit all her movable goods to us for as long as she lives . . . and if any man violates or leads astray a girl who is a minor that man shall pay with his life and goods.

XXII. We further grant that no one can be accused of injury or murder who is prepared to prove his innocence and to remove the charge from himself as long as he is convicted in court.

XXIII. We further promise that all those who were adjudged and convicted in the last investigation conducted in behalf of our beloved lord and father (may God have his soul) and of the whole country, shall remain convicted and judged as they were, without pardon, and we shall treat them as they were judged.

XXIV. We promise that the lands, cities, market places, seigniories, and fortresses which we have acquired and subjected by war shall be annexed to Brabant forever and shall not be separated from it by any compact.

XXV. We promise that those seeking to increase or extend their boundaries in our aforesaid land shall have their demands respected even against us, as well as others.

XXVI. We further promise our good people of all the

monasteries in our aforesaid lands to maintain firm and
fast forever all their privileges and charters. . . .

[The following articles dealt with specific judicial
procedures]

XXX. We further grant that each person may safeguard his goods himself, and for this purpose he may
keep dogs with untrimmed paws, without reprehension.
. . . We further grant that everyone may hunt hares and
foxes throughout Brabant without reprehension.

XXXI. We have further granted and agreed that the
knights, squires, and the good people of our cities who
have settled in Brabant shall be able to hunt, without
reprehension, any kind of wild beast throughout Brabant. . . .

XXXIV. We have further promised, sworn, confirmed,
and ratified for all our good people, of the cities, market-
places, monasteries, and all our aforesaid land all their
freedoms, charters, and especially the Charter of Cortenberg and the French Charter, as well as all their other
charters, privileges, customs, usages, and traditions which
they possess, just as they have been sealed, handed down,
and employed, and which are to be maintained firm and
fast forever by us, our heirs, and successors, without
violation or enfringement of any kind; and we promise the
good, righteous, and true men and women that no power
or force may be used against them.

And we wish and desire that all these aforesaid points,
articles, and decisions shall be kept and shall remain forever firm and fast without interruption, as we have
granted, promised, and sworn on the Holy Bible to our
aforesaid good people, their heirs, and successors. . . .
If we, our heirs, or successors should act or cause action
against any of these aforesaid points, articles, and decisions, in all or in part, howsoever and in whatever
manner it may be, we agree and authorize our aforesaid
good people that they shall not serve us, or our heirs,
or successors, or be subject to us until we have restored
these points and articles to them and desist completely.

In witness and confirmation of all these aforesaid
matters, we have hung our great seal to these present
letters, and to endow them with greater authority for our
citizens, we have requested and urged our beloved and

faithful lords . . . as well as our magistrates and knights
in Brabant to attach their seals to these present letters, in
acknowledgment and witness of all these aforesaid matters,
points, and articles. . . .

— Reading No. 5* —

THE PACIFICATION OF GHENT, NOVEMBER 8, 1576⁵

*This often quoted but rarely seen document is above
all a lasting monument to the extraordinary statesmanship
of William of Orange. The Pacification of Ghent could
have become the founding charter of the United Low
Countries, as it was meant to be, but circumstances and
momentous forces willed it otherwise. Within a decade
the Low Countries were finally and lastingly split. Yet the
concept of voluntary union, first clearly stated in this
document, has survived and is revitalized today.*

✔   ✔   ✔

To all those who shall see or hear these letters read,
greetings. As the lands up here have fallen during the
last nine or ten years into great misery and affliction as a
result of civil war, of the arrogant and harsh rule of the
Spaniards and their adherents, of their violence, their
pillaging, and other disorders, to prevent and to bring to
an end all further troubles, oppression, and ruin of the
aforesaid lands by means of a lasting peace and pacification there assembled at Breda in February, 1574 deputies
and commissioners of His Majesty and the Lord Prince
of Orange, together with the Estates of Holland, Zeeland,

---

* The translation is by Professor McDonnell.
⁵ A. S. de Blécourt and N. Japikse, eds., *Klein Plakkaatboek
van Nederland* (Groningen, 1919), pp. 113-117.

and their associates. . . . The Estates up here, with the consent of the aforesaid commissioners, have been obliged to take up arms to prevent total ruin and in order that the inhabitants of these Netherlands, being united by a firm peace and agreement, may be able as one to drive out the aforesaid Spaniards and their adherents as destroyers of the said lands and to restore to the said subjects the enjoyment of ancient rights, privileges, customs, and liberties by means of which their industry and prosperity can once again flourish.

Therefore in the earlier assembly of aforesaid lords, appointed to govern the lands, the peace negotiations begun at Breda, for the honor of God and the service of His Majesty, have been resumed by the prelates, nobles, cities and members . . . representing the Estates of the said [Belgian] lands and the Lord Prince of Orange, the Estates of Holland, Zeeland, and their associates. . . . [They] have drawn up this Treaty and conclude[d] between the aforesaid parties and lands a perpetual and firm peace, union, and alliance, with the following provisions and conditions:

I. That all offenses, injuries, crimes, and damages incurred as a result of the troubles, among the inhabitants of the provinces included in the present Treaty, in whatever place or manner they may be, shall be pardoned, forgotten, and considered as not having taken place; at no time will they be mentioned or any one be charged with them.

II. Wherefore, the aforesaid Estates of Brabant, Flanders, Hainault, etc., as well as the said Lord Prince and the Estates of Holland and Zeeland together with their associates, promise henceforth to maintain . . . unconditionally and in good faith among the inhabitants of the country a firm and inviolable friendship and peace, and to help one another in such matters at all times and in all cases with counsel and deed, goods and blood, and above all, to expel from the lands and to keep outside the Spanish soldiers and other foreigners and strangers who have tried . . . to kill the lords and nobles, to appropriate to themselves the wealth of the lands, and to reduce and maintain the state in perpetual servitude. To provide whatever is necessary to resist all those who wish to oppose them in this matter, the aforesaid confederates and allies also promise to show themselves ready and willing to bear all necessary and reasonable contributions and exactions.

III. It is agreed, moreover, as soon as the Spaniards and their adherents depart and when all matters are settled and secure, that both parties shall be bound to make possible and promote the convocation and assembly of the States-General . . . to arrange the affairs of the lands in general and in particular, both with regard to the teaching and exercise of religion in Holland, Zeeland, Bommel, and associated places, and for the restitution of the fortresses, artillery, boats, and other matters belonging to the King, which during the aforesaid troubles have been seized by those of Holland and Zeeland, or on the other hand, according as one will find to be expedient for the service of His Majesty and for the prosperity and union of the lands. This shall be done without opposition and without on either side hindrance, delay, or procrastination, whether with regard to the ordinances, declarations, and resolutions which shall be made or in the execution of those, whatever they may be, to which both parties shall submit entirely and in good faith.

IV. That henceforth the inhabitants and subjects of either side in every province up here, of whatever estate, position, or standing they may be, will be able to work, come and go, live, and trade everywhere, as merchants or otherwise, in full freedom and security, with the understanding that no one . . . will be allowed to engage in any activity, outside the aforesaid lands of Holland, Zeeland, and allied places, against the public peace and security, above all against the Roman Catholic religion and its practices; or to injure anyone, or to disturb anyone with words or deeds . . . on pain of being punished as disturbers of the public peace, in order to set an example to others.

V. And yet, in order that no one will be easily subject to prosecution, arrest, or danger, all placards [ordinances] heretofore prepared and published on the matter of heresy, together with the criminal ordinances promulgated and enforced by the Duke of Alva, shall be suspended until it has been ordained otherwise by the States-

General, with the understanding that no prejudice will ensue, as has been stated above.

VI. That our lord the Prince shall remain admiral-general of the seas and stadholder of His Majesty in Holland, Zeeland, Bommel, and associated places in order to command there in all matters as is now being done, with the same officers, justiciaries, and magistrates, without any modification or innovation; unless it is with his consent and approval, and this over the cities and places which His Excellency holds at present, until it shall be ordained otherwise by the States-General after the departure of the Spaniards.

VII. With regard to the cities and places, included in the commission of His Majesty the King and received by him, but which are not at present under the competence and obedience of His Excellency, this point shall remain in abeyance for the time being until the said cities and places shall have joined in this union and accord with the other Estates. . . .

VIII. Meanwhile no placards, ordinances, edicts, or declarations shall take effect in the aforesaid lands and cities, governed by the aforesaid Lord Prince except those which have been approved or reviewed by His Excellency, or by the Council, magistrates, or local officers, without prejudice to the jurisdiction of the Grand Council of His Majesty at a suitable time.

IX. It is hereby stipulated that all prisoners detained because of the past troubles . . . shall be released without the payment of ransom or the expenses of imprisonment except in cases where the ransom has been paid in advance or an agreement or settlement has been made in this matter.

X. Furthermore it is understood that the said Lord Prince and all other[s] . . . of whatever estate, position, or standing, as well as their widows, dowagers, children and heirs, on either side, shall be restored in their goods, name, and reputation. . . . To this end all defaults, contumacies, arrests, sentences, seizures, and executions, given and made since the outbreak of the troubles of the year 1566, both with regard to religion and for taking up arms with the dire consequences resulting therefrom, are rescinded, revoked, and annulled. . . .

[Articles XI and XII dealt with the rights of specific persons.]

XIII. And the columns, trophies, inscriptions, and other tokens erected by the Duke of Alva, to the dishonor and disgrace of those who have been named above, and all others, shall be destroyed.

[The following articles are concerned with various property claims.]

XX. That all the prelates and other ecclesiastical persons whose abbeys, dioceses, foundations, and residences are located outside Holland and Zeeland and nevertheless are beneficed in the said lands, shall be returned to the possession and enjoyment of their said goods, as described above with respect to the laity.

XXI. But as for the other clergymen who took their vows or were provided with prebends in the two aforesaid provinces and their associates and have withdrawn from them, seeing that most of their goods have been alienated, we shall henceforth give them reasonable maintenance with those who have remained, or else they shall be permitted to use their goods at the choice of the Estates; all shall be arranged by the States-General provisionally and in anticipation of further claims.

XXII. Furthermore it is agreed that all donations, exheredations, and other dispositions *inter vivos vel causa mortis,* made by private persons, and by which the real heirs have been rejected, wronged, and disinherited because of the aforesaid troubles or religion, shall, by virtue of the present agreement, be considered rescinded and invalid.

XXIII. And as those of Holland and Zeeland, in order better to provide for the expenses of the war, have placed at high price all gold and silver specie which they could not spend in other provinces without considerable loss, it is stipulated that the deputies of the States-General shall consider as soon as possible a general measure in order to equalize the price of the aforesaid monies, as best as can be done for the maintenance of this Union, and the facility of reciprocal trade.

XXIV. And as for the representation made by the deputies of Holland and Zeeland in order that the generality of all the Low Countries should assume as their burden all debts which our lord the Prince has incurred for his two expeditions and the raising of his great armies, in consequence of which Holland and Zeeland as well as the provinces and cities which surrendered at the time of the last campaign have been kept united, as they say; this point has been proposed and left to the discretion and determination of the said States-General to which, after all matters have been settled, report and remonstrance shall be made in order that the proper action will be taken.

XXV. In this general accord and pacification shall not be included, in order to derive benefit from it, the lands, seignories, and cities adhering to the opposite view until they shall have effectively joined and united in this confederation, which they can do when it pleases them.

This Treaty and negotiations for peace in consequence of the willingness, agreement, and approbation of the lords commissioned for the government of the said lands . . . the aforesaid deputies by virtue of their power and commission have promised and sworn to observe, maintain, and execute unceasingly . . . to have them respectively ratified, sworn to, signed and sealed on either side by the prelates, nobles, cities, and other members of the aforesaid lands, and especially by the said Lord of Orange, in general and particular, and this within the month which follows the pleasure of each. In witness of what precedes the aforesaid deputies have signed the present document in the city hall of Ghent on November 8, 1576.

THE DECLARATION OF THE STATES-GENERAL OF THE UNITED PROVINCES, SETTING FORTH THAT PHILIP II HAD FORFEITED HIS RIGHT OF SOVEREIGNTY OVER THE SAID PROVINCES. THE HAGUE, JULY 26, 1581 [6]

This declaration of independence in its unsophisticated terms is one of the most impressive in the history of man. Long before the Americans and other Western peoples set forth their reasons for the renunciation of existing allegiances, the Dutch had taken an unprecedented step of courage and rebellion. Economic, religious, and political motivations combined to force this bold decision.

✦   ✦   ✦

The States-General of the United Provinces of the Low Countries, to all whom it may concern, do by these Presents send greetings:

As is apparent to all that a prince is constituted by God to be ruler of a people, to defend them from oppression and violence as the shepherd his sheep; and whereas God did not create the people slaves to their prince to obey his commands, whether right or wrong, but rather the prince for the sake of the subjects (without which he could not be prince) to govern them according to equity . . . and even at the hazard of life to defend

---

[6] *Old South Leaflets* (Boston [1896]), Vol. 3. The translation reprinted in this series is that of Lord Somers.

and preserve them. And when he does not behave thus, but, on the contrary, oppresses them, seeking opportunities to infringe on their ancient customs and privileges, exacting from them slavish compliance, then he is no longer a prince but a tyrant and the subjects are to regard him in no other way. And particularly when this is done deliberately, unauthorized by the States, they may not only disallow his authority but legally proceed to the choice of another prince for their defence. This is the only method left for subjects whose humble petitions and remonstrances could never soften their prince . . . and this is what the law of nature dictates for the defence of liberty, which we ought to transmit to posterity, even at the hazard of our lives. And this we have seen done frequently . . . and [is] more justifiable in our land, which has always been governed according to our ancient privileges, which are expressed in the oath taken by the prince at his admission to the government; for most of the Provinces receive their prince upon certain conditions, which he swears to maintain and which, if the prince violates them, do not make him any longer sovereign. Now thus it was with the King of Spain after the demise of the emperor, his father, Charles the Fifth . . . forgetting the services performed by the subjects of these countries . . . by whose valor he obtained such glorious and memorable victories . . . [and who] did rather hearken to the counsel of those Spaniards about him, who had conceived a secret hate for this land and its liberty because they could not enjoy posts of honor and high employment here under the States as in . . . other countries under the king's dominion. . . . The King of Spain, following these evil counsellors, sought by all the means possible to reduce this country . . . to slavery . . . having first, under the mask of religion, endeavored to establish new bishops in the largest . . . cities, endowing and incorporating them with the richest abbeys. . . . By this incorporation the said bishops . . . would have held first place and vote in the assembly of the States . . . and by the addition of the said canons he would have introduced the Spanish inquisition, which has been always as dreadful and detested in the Provinces as the worst of slavery. . . . But notwithstanding the many remonstrances made to the king both by the Provinces and

particular towns . . . as well as by some principal lords
. . . and in particular by the Baron de Montigny [Count
Hoorn] and the Earl of Egmont, who with the approbation of the Duchess of Parma, then governess of the Low
Countries, . . . were sent several times to Spain upon
this affair. And, although the king had by fair words given
them grounds to hope that their request should be com-
plied with, yet by his letters ordered the contrary, soon
after expressly commanding . . . to admit the new
bishops immediately . . . to hold the court of inquisition
. . . to obey and follow the decrees and ordinances of
the Council of Trent, which in many articles are destruc-
tive of the privileges of the country. This having come
to the knowledge of the people gave just occasion to great
uneasiness . . . and lessened the affection they had
always borne toward the king and his predecessors. And
especially after seeing that he did not only seek to tyran-
nize their persons and estates but also their consciences for
which they believed themselves accountable to God only.
Upon that occasion in the year 1566, the chief of the
nobility in compassion with the poor people, exhibited a
certain remonstrance in form of a petition . . . in order
to appease them and prevent public disturbances that it
would please His Majesty . . . to soften the said points,
especially in regard to the rigorous inquisition and capital
punishment in matters of religion. . . . The king instead
of . . . redressing the grievances . . . did by advice of
the Spanish Council declare all those who were concerned
in preparing the said remonstrance to be rebels and
guilty of high treason and to be punished by death . . .
and, what is more, . . . did soon after imprison and put
to death the said lords [Egmont and Montigny] and con-
fiscated their estates, contrary to the law of nations. . . .
And although the said disturbances, which happened at
the aforementioned occasion, were now appeased . . .
and many friends of liberty were either banished or
subdued, . . . he has, at the instigation of the Council of
Spain . . . sent the Duke of Alva with a powerful army
to suppress this land, who for his inhumane cruelties is
looked upon as one of its greatest enemies . . . ; he immediately garrisoned the principal towns and castles and
caused fortresses and citadels to be built in the great
cities to awe them into subjection and very courteously

sent for the chiefs of nobility . . . under the pretense of
taking their advice. . . . And those who believed his
letters were seized . . . contrary to law . . . imprisoned
and prosecuted as criminals before him who had no right,
nor could be a competent judge . . . and at last . . .
sentenced them to death. The others, better acquainted
with Spanish hypocrisy, residing in foreign countries, were
declared outlaws. . . . In order to impoverish the subjects and to incapacitate them to hinder his design, . . .
he [Alva] began to alter the course of justice after Spanish
fashion, obliquely contrary to our privileges; and, imagin-
ing at last he had nothing more to fear he endeavored by
main force to settle a tax called the tenth penny on
merchandise and manufacture to the total ruin of these
countries. . . . Soon after the Provinces of Holland and
Zeeland revolted for the most part, putting themselves
under the protection of the Prince of Orange. . . . [The
document then gives an account of the conduct of Spanish
troops and continues]. . . . The aforesaid Prince of
Orange, in conjunction with the Provinces of Holland and
Zeeland [decided] . . . unanimously to declare war
against the Spaniards as their common enemy, to drive
them out of the country; at the same time, like good
subjects, making good use of all proper applications,
humbly petitioned the king to have compassion on account
of the calamities already suffered. . . . The king would
have us believe that all this was transacted without his
knowledge, and that he intended to punish the authors
[of the suppressions]. . . . And yet he not only neglected
to do us justice by punishing the offenders; on the contrary, it is plain that all was done by orders concerted in
the Council of Spain. . . . And the more to blind his
subjects, he sent at the same time Don Juan, his natural
brother . . . to govern these countries, who under pretense of approving the Treaty of Ghent . . . of settling
the public peace, and of re-establishing ancient liberties,
endeavored to divide the said estates in order to enslave
one after another. . . . All these considerations give us
more than sufficient reason to renounce the King of Spain,
and seek some other powerful and more gracious prince to
take us under his protection; and, more especially, as
these countries have been for twenty years abandoned to
disturbance and oppression by their king, during which

time the inhabitants were not treated as subjects, but
enemies, forcibly enslaved by their own governors.

. . . At last we found by experience that nothing would
be obtained of the king by prayers and treaties, which
latter he made use of to divide and weaken the Provinces, that he might easier execute his plan rigorously,
. . . which afterwards plainly appeared by certain proclamations and prescription . . . by virtue of which we
and all officers and inhabitants of the United Provinces
with all our friends are declared rebels, and as such, have
forfeited our lives and estates. Thus by rendering us odious
to all, he might interrupt our commerce, likewise reducing
us to despair offering a great sum to anyone who would
assassinate the Prince of Orange. So having no hope of
reconciliation, and finding no other remedy, we have,
agreeable to the laws of nature in our own defence, and
for the maintenance of the rights, privileges, and liberties
of our countrymen, wives, and children, and ultimate
posterity . . . been constrained to renounce allegiance
to the King of Spain and to pursue such methods as
appear to us most likely to secure our ancient liberties
and privileges. Know all men by these Presents that,
being reduced to the last extremity, . . . we have
unanimously and deliberately declared, and do by these
Presents declare, that the King of Spain has forfeited,
ipso jure, all hereditary right to the sovereignty of these
countries. . . . In consequence whereof we also declare
all officers, judges, lords, gentlemen, vassals, and all other
inhabitants of this country of whatsoever condition and
quality, to be henceforth free from all oaths and obligations made to the King of Spain as sovereign of these
countries. . . . We command and order all justiciaries,
officers, and all whom it may concern not to make henceforth use of the name, titles, great or privy seal of the
King of Spain. . . . And instead of the king's seal aforesaid, they shall make use of our great seal. . . . And in
affairs concerning the administration of justice, and
transactions peculiar to each Province, the provincial
council and other councils of the country shall use
respectively the name, title, and seal of the said Province.
. . . Moreover, we order and command that henceforth
no money shall be stamped with the name, title, or arms
of the King of Spain in any of these Provinces. . . . We

order likewise and command the president, and other lords
of the privy council and all other chancellors, presidents,
and lords . . . judges and officers . . . that they shall
take a new oath to the Estates of that country on whose
jurisdiction they depend . . . We farther command the
president and members of the privy council . . . justiciaries and officers whom it may concern . . . to cause
this our ordinance to be published and proclaimed
throughout their respective jurisdictions . . . and for
better maintaining all and every article hereof, we give to
all and every of you, by express command, full power and
authority. In witness whereof we have hereunto set our
hands and seals, dated in our assembly at The Hague,
the six and twentieth day of July, 1581, endorsed by
order of the States-General. . . .

— Reading No. 7 —

TREATY OF PEACE BETWEEN PHILIP IV, KING OF SPAIN, AND THE UNITED PROVINCES OF THE LOW COUNTRIES. MUNSTER, JANUARY 30, 1648[7]

*After eighty years of war the Treaty of Munster finally
confirmed Dutch independence. The same treaty also
separated the northern and southern Low Countries,
which for centuries thereafter underwent a different
development. Yet even in this separation a certain amount
of freedom of crossing into the northern and southern*

[7] *A General Collection of Treaties, Manifestos, Contracts of
Marriage, Renunciations, and other Publick Papers from
1495 to the Present Time* (London, 1713), II, 335-367.

provinces respectively and retaining property there was preserved.

          1   *1*   *1*

In the Name and to the Glory of God, be it known to all Men, That after the long Course of bloody Wars, which have so many years afflicted the People, Subjects, Kingdoms and Countries in the Obedience of the Lords the King of *Spain,* and the States General of the *United Provinces* of the *Low Countries;* the said Lords, the King and States being touch'd with Christian Compassion, and desirous to put an end to the publick Calamities . . . and in order to change the pernicious Effects thereof into those most desirable ones of a good and sincere Pacification on both sides . . . praying and beseeching all other Christian Princes and Potentates to suffer themselves to be prevail'd upon . . . to have a Compassion for and Aversion to the Miseries, Ruins, and Disorders which this present Scourge of War has made us feel so long and so severely. . . .

I. In the first place the said Lord the King declares and acknowledges, That the said Lords the States General of the *Low Countries,* and all the respective Provinces thereof, together with all the associated Countries . . . are Free and Sovereign States, Provinces and Countries . . . and that neither at this time, nor *in futurum,* he shall ever make any Pretensions to them for himself, or for his Heirs and Successors: and that in consequence thereof he is content to treat with the said Lord of the States . . . and agree upon a perpetual Peace. . . .

II. That the said Peace shall be good, firm, faithful and inviolable and that from henceforth shall cease all Acts of Hostility . . . between . . . the King and the States General. . . .

III. Each shall remain effectively in the Possession and Enjoyment of the Countries, Town, Forts, Lands and Dominions which he holds and possesses at present. . . .

IV. And the Subjects and Inhabitants of the Countries of the said Lords . . . shall entertain all good Correspondence among themselves . . . ; they may likewise remain in and frequent one another Countries, and there exercise their Traffick and Commerce in all Safety . . .

V. The Navigation and Trade to the *East* and *West Indies,* shall be kept up according. . . .

[The following articles dealt specifically with both these regions.]

VIII. The Subjects and Inhabitants of the Countries of the foresaid Lords . . . trading to one another's Countries, shall not be oblig'd to pay greater Duties and Imports, than the respective Subjects Natives of the Countries. . . .

IX. The said Lords the King and the States shall not raise, without their respective Limits, any Duties or Gabels for Entry, Parting or any other Account. . . .

X. The Subjects of the said Lords . . . shall respectively in one another's Countries enjoy the antient Privilege of the Customs, whereof they have been in peaceable possession before the Commencement of the War.

XI. Society, Conversation and Commerce among the respective Subjects shall not be hinder'd. . . .

XII. And from the Day of the Conclusion and Ratification of this Peace, the King shall cause the raising of all Customs. . . .

XIII. The white boil'd Salt coming from the *United Provinces* into those of his said Majesty, shall be there receiv'd and admitted, without being charg'd with higher Duties than Bay Salt. . . .

XIV. The Rivers of the *Escaut,* [Scheldt] as also the Canals of *Sas, Zwyn,* and other Mouths of Rivers disimboguing themselves there, shall be kept shut on the side of the Lord of the States.

XV. The Ships and Commodities entering into and coming out of the Harbours of *Flanders* shall be respectively charg'd by the . . . King with all such Imports and other Duties, as are laid upon Commodities going and coming along the *Escaut.* . . .

XVI. The Hans[e] Towns . . . shall enjoy all the same Rights, Franchises, Privileges and Immunities, which by the present Treaty are granted . . . And the said Subjects . . . of the *United Provinces* of the *Low Countries,* shall reciprocally enjoy all the same Rights. . . .

XVII. The Subjects . . . of the Countries of the said Lords, the States, shall also have the same Security and

Freedom in the Countries . . . of the King, that has been granted to the Subjects of the King of *Great Britain*. . . .

XVIII. The . . . King shall make . . . all necessary Provision, that honourable Places may be appointed for the Interment of such Bodies of such Subjects of the Lords of the States, as shall happen to die in any Place under the Obedience of the . . . King.

XIX. The Subjects . . . of the . . . King, coming into the Countries . . . of the . . . States[-General], shall be oblig'd, with regard to publick Exercise of Religion, to govern and behave themselves with all Modesty. . . . And the same shall be done . . . by the Subjects . . . of the said Lords the States, coming into the Lands of the . . . King.

XX. The Merchants, Masters of Ships . . . Merchandices, Commodities . . . may not be seiz'd. . . .

XXI. Certain Judges shall be appointed on both sides in equal Number, in form of the *Chambre Mipartie*, who shall sit in the *Low Countries*. . . . And if the said Judges perceive that any Excesses are committed on either side . . . they shall regulate and moderate the said Excesses. . . .

XXII. . . . nor shall any Letters of Mark or Reprisal be granted, but upon Cognizance of the Cause, and in cases allowed by Imperial Laws. . . .

XXIII. It shall not be lawful to come ashore, enter or stop at the Ports . . . or Roads of one another with Men of War and Soldiers, in such numbers as may cause suspicion, without . . . Leave and Permission. . . .

XXIV. Such whose Goods have been seiz'd . . . upon occasion of the War, or their Heirs . . . shall recover and take possession of the said Goods . . . in virtue of this Treaty. . . .

XXV. This shall also take place in the Profits arising to the Heirs of the late Lord, Prince *William of Orange*. . . .

XXVI. In which are also meant to be comprehended the other Goods and rights in the Countries of *Burgundy* and *Charolais*. . . .

XXVII. In like manner are meant to be comprehended the Goods and Rights, which, after the Expiration of the Twelve Years Truce, were adjudg'd to the late *John* Count of *Nassau*. . . .

XXIX. If any Difficulty should arise concerning the Restitution of the Goods and Rights that are to be restor'd, the Judg[e] of the Place shall cause Restitution to be made without delay. . . .

XXX. The Subjects . . . of the *United Low-Countries* may, every where in the Lands . . . of . . . the King employ such Advocates . . . and Agents as they shall think proper . . . and Subjects of . . . the King coming into . . . the States shall have the same Assistance.

XXXI. If the Fisque [Treasury] has sold any of the Goods of either side, those to whom they should apertain by virtue of this Treaty shall be oblig'd to be satisfy'd with the Interest at the rate of 16 *per Cent.* to be paid every Year by those who possess the said Goods. . . .

[The following articles were concerned with restitution procedures, including church properties, public buildings, the possessions of William of Orange, etc.]

LI. The said Lords the King and the States shall appoint . . . Officers and Magistrates . . . in the Towns and Garrisons, which by this present Treaty are to be given up to the Proprietors in possession.

LII. The upper Quarter of *Guelder* shall be exchang'd for an Equivalent; and in case that Equivalent cannot be agreed upon, the matter shall be refer'd to the *Chambre Mipartie*. . . .

LIII. The . . . King obliges himself effectually to procure the Continuation and Observation of the Neutrality, Amity, and good Neighborhood of his Imperial Majesty and the Empire with . . . the States.

[Articles LIV-LVII dealt again with claims to property.]

LVIII. No new Forts may be made in the *Low Countries* on either side. . . .

LXIX. Neither the Lords of the House of *Nassau*, nor Count *John Albert* of *Solms*, Governor of *Maestricht*, may be prosecuted or molested. . . .

LX. If any Contravention should be made to the Treaty . . . without the Command of the . . . King and the States, the Damage shall be repair'd in the same Place where the Contravention shall have been made. . . .

LXI. All Disinherisons and Dispositions made in the Heat and Fury of War shall be declar'd null, and held as not made. . . .

LXII. The Subjects . . . of the Countries of . . . the King and the States . . . are declar'd capable of succeeding to one another. . . .

LXIII. All Prisoners of War shall be delivere'd up, on both sides, without paying any Ransom. . . .

LXIV. The Payment of Arrears of Contributions which shall remain unpaid from the Conclusion of the Treaty . . . shall be regulated . . . by those of both sides who shall have the Superintendance of Contributions.

[L]XV. And whatever shall be propos'd or alleg'd on either side . . . shall not be turn'd or interpreted to the Advantage or Prejudice of any directly or indirectly. . . .

LXVI. The respective Inhabitants . . . shall really enjoy the Effect . . . of the twelve Years Truce now expired . . . [1609-1621].

LXVII. The Limits and Bounds in *Flanders* and elsewhere shall be regulated in such sort as shall be found just. . . .

LXVIII. On the part . . . of . . . the King of *Spain,* the Forts nam'd here l'Écluse shall be demolished. . . .

LXIX. All the Registers, Charters, Letters, Archives and Papers . . . concerning any of the respective *United Provinces* . . . at . . . any Place under the Obedience of the . . . King shall be deliver'd *bona fide* to those who shall have a Commission from the said respective Provinces. . . .

LXX. The Jurisdiction over the Waters shall be left to the Town of l'Écluse [Sluis], as appertains to it.

LXXI. The Dike that crosses the River *Soute* . . . shall be . . . open'd.

[The following articles referred to persons and cities named as coming within the purview of the Treaty as well as with specific persons who advanced restitution claims.]

LXXV. And to the end that the present Treaty may be better observ'd, . . . the King and the States respectively promise to use their Endeavours . . . to render the [water] Passages free . . . and secure from all Incursions of Pirats. . . .

LXXVI. They promise moreover not to do anything contrary to or in prejudice of the present Treaty. . . .

LXXVII. The present Treaty shall be ratify'd . . . within the Term of two Months.

LXXVIII. . . . in the meanwhile the Affairs of both

sides shall continue in the same State and Condition they shall be found at the Conclusion of the present Treaty. . . .

LXXIX. The said Treaty shall be publish'd everywhere . . . after the Ratifications . . . and from thenceforth all Acts of Hostility shall cease.

— Reading No. 8 —

TREATY OF UNION AND ESTABLISHMENT OF THE SOVEREIGN CONGRESS OF THE UNITED BELGIAN STATES. BRUSSELS, JANUARY 11, 1790 [8]

In this half-forgotten document the Belgian provinces declared themselves for the first time free and independent. But differently from such declarations of independence as that of the United States, the Belgian declaration is rather conservative. Medieval liberties are frequently referred to. It is of special interest to compare the Belgian and Dutch declarations of independence since there are a number of striking parallels.

✔   ✔   ✔

After the death of the Dowager Empress and Queen Maria-Theresa of Austria, the peoples which form today the United States of the Low Countries, have recognized as their sovereign the Emperor Joseph II . . . and have submitted to his empire; but under reservations and with the express stipulation that the constitution of these

[8] M. P. Verhaegen, *Recueil des Ordonnances des Pays-Bas Austrichiens, Troisième Série, 1700-1794* (Brussels, 1914), XIII, 418-421.

provinces, in force since ancient times, [must be preserved].

These stipulations and reservations, contained in the inaugural pact, were older than the House which governs the country and born, so to speak, with the nation itself. They were also agreed and solemnly sworn to, and nothing lacked in the treaty, which the people . . . made according to the custom with the prince.

The complete conservation of the ancient Catholic, Apostolic, and Roman religion; the maintenance of the constitution, the liberties, franchises, customs, and uses which were contained in the charters and consecrated by the immemorial possession of the nation and among which Brabant recalls above all her Joyeuse Entrée; all this was agreed to and promised upon the fidelity of an oath.

The inhabitants have it all the more at heart since they have made for a long time a pleasant habit of regarding these matters as forming essentially their constitution and [of regarding] this constitution as the rampart of their liberties, which they safeguard with their fortunes.

However, in spite of the oath, so positive [on the part] of the sovereign . . . , in spite of the representations so often reiterated by all the classes of the State [and] touching upon countless infractions committed against this pact, the sovereign followed for several years a constant course which aimed at nothing less than to change everything, to innovate without interruption, and to deprive the inhabitants of a constitution which was so dear to them and of which he could not despoil them without injustice, without violating his oath.

One has already seen appear successively a multitude of edicts which attack religion in . . . its morale and rites, in its dogma, and in its ministers. The courts of the nation have been overthrown; the laws changed arbitrarily or infringed upon; property, personal freedom, which the Belgians are so concerned with, are no longer sheltered from unconstitutional maneuvers. The laws are silent, having become impotent before the sword of the military; the old customs are everywhere altered or revoked; a new order has been substituted for the old one and replaced it by the variable and arbitrary whims of the prince or of those who govern in his name and act under his authority. Such has been the extent of our ills; they have become irremediable. The government, not content to brace itself against all remonstrations, closed by a new and last coup the door against the remonstrances themselves, by abrogating the Joyeuse Entrée, the ancient rights and fundamental laws of the provinces, abolishing together with the constitution the assembly of deputies in these provinces, which were up to now the ordinary organs of representation. . . .

Finally, the pact, which ceases to bind us because it ceases to be reciprocal, was formally broken on the part of the sovereign. And what remains after this for the people if not the natural and imprescriptible law, . . . to oppose violence by force and to reassume authority, which one has entrusted solely for the common well-being and with so many precautions under the stipulations and reservations thus expressed?

This has been done: and it has been done according to these principles that the several provinces are declared free and independent. The heavens have visibly blessed an enterprise formed under such auspices; Europe and humanity have applauded its successes. But it is not everything to have obtained successes; it is necessary to think of consolidating them. . . .

For these reasons the Belgian states have agreed on the following points and articles after having tightened the ancient bonds of a close union and of an enduring friendship.

FIRST ARTICLE. All the provinces unite and confederate themselves under the name of the United Belgian States.

ARTICLE 2. These provinces in common agreement unite and concentrate the sovereign powers [in their hands]; confine and restrict themselves, however, to the following objects: common defense, power to make peace and war and, in consequence thereof, to the levy and maintenance of a national army . . . , contract alliances, offensive as well as defensive; nominate, send, and receive ministers . . . , all this by the sole authority of the power thus assumed and without any recourse to the respective provinces. One has agreed at the same time on the influence which each province will have through its deputies in the deliberations and on the points enumerated in the present Treaty.

ARTICLE 3. To exercise the sovereign power they [the

provinces] create and establish a congress of deputies from each of the provinces under the title of sovereign Congress of the United Belgian States.

ARTICLE 4. [Since] the provinces above mentioned profess now and are willing to profess forever the Catholic, Apostolic, and Roman religion and wish to preserve inviolate the unity of the Church, the Congress will observe and maintain the ancient rapport with the Holy See both in the nomination and presentation of subjects of the said provinces to archbishoprics or bishoprics . . . and in all other matters conforming to the principles of the Catholic Apostolic Roman religion, the concordats and liberties of the Belgian Church.

ARTICLE 5. The Congress alone shall have power to coin money with the imprint of the United Belgian States and to fix standards and values.

ARTICLE 6. The provinces of the union furnish the necessary outlay for the exercise of the sovereign powers attributed to the Congress. . . .

ARTICLE 7. Each province retains and reserves all other rights of sovereignty, legislation, liberty, [and] independence as well as all those powers, jurisdiction and rights whatsoever, which are not expressly and collectively delegated to the sovereign Congress.

ARTICLE 8. It is moreover irrevocably agreed that in regard to difficulties which could arise, be it at the occasion of the common contribution, be it about any subject of discussion, be it between a province and the Congress, or of the Congress with a province, or of a province with a province, the Congress will endeavor to terminate them in a friendly way; and if such friendly arrangement cannot take place each province shall nominate one person at the request of one or the other party who will examine the case summarily and judge it. The Congress will have the power of execution, and if the judgment is against the Congress, the latter shall be obliged to submit.

ARTICLE 9. The United States oblige themselves to help each other in the closest possible manner, and if one province is attacked, they all will make common cause and defend together with all their forces the province thus attacked.

ARTICLE 10. No province is free to make any alliance or treaty whatsoever with another power without the consent of the Congress; and the individual provinces cannot unite themselves, ally, or contract in any way without the consent of the Congress. However, the province of Flanders can reunite itself with West Flanders on condition that each will have their particular deputies in Congress. . . . The deputies of the one can never be at the same time the deputies of the other.

ARTICLE 11. This union shall be stable, perpetual, [and] irrevocable. Neither a single province nor several, not even in a plurality, shall be free to break this union or to separate from each other under any pretext or for any motive whatsoever.

ARTICLE 12. It has also been agreed that civil and military power . . . shall never be bestowed upon the same person and that a person having seat and vote in Congress cannot be employed in military service. . . .

To this effect all the States composing the union in general and each member in particular, of all those who will partake in the session of the Congress, all councillors and members of provincial councils, all magistrates, and generally all judges and civilian officers promise and swear to the exact and loyal observation of this union and all and each of its points. Thus concluded, made, and ordered at Brussels in the general assembly of the United Belgian States by the undersigned deputies of the respective States under the ratification of their constituents. The 11th of January of the year 1790, at 2:00 A.M.

— Reading No. 9 —

THE FUNDAMENTAL LAW (GRONDWET) OF THE KINGDOM OF THE NETHERLANDS, AUGUST 24, 1815[9]

The Fundamental Law became the constitutional foundation on which the kingdom of the Netherlands has rested since 1815. Modifications have been introduced and, if they substantially changed the character of the 1815 constitution, have been given here in italics and are taken from the latest revision of the Grondwet *in 1956. As will be seen, however, in many basic aspects the* Grondwet *has remained unchanged. This attests to the inherent qualities of the Fundamental Law as much as to the political wisdom of the Dutch. On the other hand, the fact should not be overlooked that the 1815 constitution was the handiwork of conservative statesmen and that it combined eighteenth-century concepts of strong monarchical government with the traditional constitutional and institutional rights of the Dutch people as well as with ideas stemming from the French Revolution.*

✦   ✦   ✦

Chapter I—Of the Kingdom and Its Inhabitants

article 1. The Kingdom of the Netherlands whose borders are fixed by the Treaty concluded between the

[9] Great Britain, Foreign Office, *British and Foreign State Papers, 1815-1816* (London, 1838), III, 16-42. The articles in italics are translated from *Staatsblad van het Koninkrijk der Nederlanden* (The Hague, 1956). *Stb. 472,* pp. 1211-1224. The text of the Fundamental Law of 1815 has been translated from the French.

powers of Europe assembled at the Congress of Vienna
. . . is composed of the following provinces:

North Brabant	Zeeland
South Brabant	Namur
Limburg	Antwerp
Gelderland	Utrecht
Liége	Frisia
East Flanders	Overyssel
West Flanders	Groningen
Hainaut	Drenthe
Holland	

The Grand Duchy of Luxembourg as it has been de-
limited by the Treaty of Vienna, having been placed
under the same sovereignty as the Kingdom of the
Netherlands, will be governed by the same Fundamental
Law, except for its relations with the German Confederation. . . .

ARTICLE 1. *The Kingdom of the Netherlands comprises
the territory of the Netherlands, Surinam, the Netherlands Antilles and Netherlands New Guinea.*

ARTICLE 2. *The Constitution shall be binding only for
the Realm in Europe, inasmuch as the contrary does not
become evident. . . .*

IV. All individuals who live in the territory of the
Kingdom, be it as inhabitants or as foreigners, have equal
claim to the protection of life and goods.

V. The exercise of civil rights is determined by law.

VI. The right to vote . . . as well as the admission to
the provincial and local administrations is regulated by
provincial and local statutes.

[The following articles deal with qualifications for state
officers.]

XI. Every person is equally admissible to employment
without distinction of rank and birth. . . .

CHAPTER II—OF THE KING

XII. The crown of the Kingdom of the Netherlands is
and remains bestowed upon his Majesty William Freder-
ick, Prince of Orange-Nassau, and in heredity to his
legitimate descendants. . . .

[The constitution then prescribes the right of succession.
Section II of this chapter deals with the civil list and the

position of the heir presumptive, while the following sections are concerned with the establishment of a regency and the procedures upon accession of a new ruler.]

ARTICLE 55. *The King shall be inviolable; the ministers shall be responsible.*

ARTICLE 56. *The executive power shall be vested in the King.* .

LVI. The King has the direction of foreign affairs, he appoints and recalls the ministers and consuls.

ARTICLE 58. *The King . . . promotes the development of an international legal order.*

LVII. The King declares war and makes peace; he informs the two chambers of the States-General . . . if he believes that this is compatible with the interests and the security of the state.

ARTICLE 59. *The King declares the Kingdom in a state of war . . . only after previous consent of the States-General . . . The King does not declare war between the Kingdom and another power as ended without the preliminary consent of the States-General.*

LVIII. To the King belongs the right to conclude and to ratify all other treaties and conventions. . . . When the treaties concluded in time of peace contain a cession or an exchange of a part of the territory of the Kingdom . . . , they are ratified by the King only after they have been approved by the States-General.

ARTICLE 60. *Agreements with other powers and international organizations shall be concluded by or with the authorization of the King . . . The agreements shall be communicated as quickly as possible to the States-General; they shall not be confirmed or become effective unless they have been approved by the States-General. . . .*

LIX. The King commands the land and sea forces . . .

LX. The supreme direction of the colonies . . . belongs exclusively to the King. [This article does not appear in the present constitution.]

LXI. The King has the supreme direction of finances. . . .

LXII. The King has the right to coin money. . . .

LXIII. The King bestows nobility. . . .

[The Grondwet then regulates the creation of orders of merit, grants of pardon, and the right of royal dispensation.]

LXIX. The King decides in all disputes which arise between two or more provinces if they cannot be terminated amicably.

LXX. The King presents to the States-General projects of law and makes to them such other propositions as he judges convenient. He sanctions or rejects the propositions which the States-General make to him.

[Section VII covers the establishment of the council of state and ministerial departments. Article LXXI stipulated that the king was to preside over the Council of State and the next article that he could dismiss ministers at will.]

Chapter III—The States-General

LXXVII. The States-General represent the nation.

LXXVIII. The States-General are formed by two Chambers.

LXXIX. One of these chambers is composed of one hundred ten members named by the provincial estates as follows. . . .

article 90. *The members of the Second Chamber are directly elected by the native Netherlanders as well as by those who are recognized by law as Netherlands subjects.* . . .

article 91. *The Second Chamber consists of one hundred fifty members.*

LXXX. The other chamber which bears the name of the First Chamber is composed of at least forty members or sixty at most, aged forty years [and above], nominated for life by the King among the persons most distinguished for the services rendered to the state by their birth or their property. . . .

article 92. *The First Chamber consists of seventy-five members. They are elected by the members of the Provincial [E]states on the basis of proportional representation.* . . .

article 101. *The members of the First Chamber shall be elected for six years. . . . One half shall retire every three years. The retiring members shall be reëligible immediately.*

LXXXI. Eligible for the Second Chamber are persons domiciled in the province in which they are nominated . . . Members elected in the same province must not be

related by blood or marriage up to the third degree.
Officers of the land and sea forces are not eligible unless
they have rank above that of Captain. [These provisions
have been withdrawn in the revised constitution.]

LXXXII. The members of this Chamber are elected for
three years [four years under the present constitution. . . .]

LXXXIII. The members of this Chamber vote in-
dividually without orders or reference to the assembly
which has nominated them.

[Subsequent articles deal with technical provisions regarding the form of oath, remuneration, appointment of
the presiding officer, etc., as well as with similar provisions
for members of the First Chamber.]

CV. The legislative powers are concurrently exercised
by the King and the States-General.

CVI. The King addresses to the Second Chamber
propositions . . .

[The following articles regulate the procedures of acceptance or rejection on the part of the chambers. In
the revised constitution Article 122 provides specifically
that the States-General have the right to make modifications in a proposal of the King.]

CXIII. The States-General have the right to make
propositions to the King. . . .

CXIV. The right to bring about a deliberation of the
States-General on a proposition to be made by the King
belongs exclusively to the members of the Second Chamber. . . .

[The final articles in this section deal with the word-
ing of the sovereign's approval or disapproval of bills
and the form by which they are changed into law.]

CXXI. The budget of the expenditures of the Kingdom
must have the consent of the States-General; it is presented by the King to the Second Chamber in ordinary
session.

CXXII. The budget is divided into two parts. . . .

CXXIII. The first part contains all the ordinary fixed
and constant expenditures. . . . These expenditures, having been approved by the States-General, are not for the
first ten years subject to an ultimate and annual consent.

ARTICLE 134. *The period* [for an approved budget]
cannot be in excess of two years.

CXXVI. The second part of the budget contains the extraordinary expenditures . . . which, above all in time of war, must be regulated according to circumstances. . . .

CXXVIII. The King shall give annually before the States-General a detailed account of the use of public funds.

ARTICLE 136. *The responsibility for the expenditures and receipts of the Realm for each service will be rendered, upon submission of the accounts approved by the Chamber of Accounts, to the legislative power.*

CHAPTER IV—OF THE PROVINCIAL [E]STATES

CXXIX. The Provincial [E]states are composed of the members elected by the three following orders: the Nobles or Equestrian Corps; the Cities; the Countryside.

CXXX. The total number of members of which the Provincial [E]states are composed and the number to be elected by each order are fixed by the King. . . .

ARTICLE 137. *The members of the Provincial [E]states will be directly elected for a stipulated number of years determined by law by the inhabitants of a province.* . . .

[The following articles regulate the mechanics of provincial elections and voting procedures.]

CXLV. The [E]states are charged with the execution of the laws relative to the protection of the different religions . . . , public instruction, administration of welfare, encouragement of agriculture, commerce, and manufacturing. . . .

CXLIX. The King can suspend or annul the acts of the Provincial [E]states if they are contrary to the laws or to the general interest.

ARTICLE 149. *The power of the King to suspend or annul resolutions of the Provincial [E]states which are in conflict with the general interest shall be regulated by law.*

CLIV. The rural administrations of seignories, districts, or villages are organized in a manner found the most convenient.

CHAPTER V—OF JUSTICE

CLXII. Justice is rendered everywhere in the name of the King.

CLXIII. There shall exist for the whole Kingdom the same civil, penal, [and] commercial code. . . .

CLXIV. The peaceable possession and enjoyment of property is guaranteed to each inhabitant.

CLXV. Disputes which have as their object property or rights derived therefrom . . . or civil rights are exclusively within the province of the courts.

ARTICLE 165. *Expropriation for public use cannot take place without a previous declaration of the law.* . . .

CLXVII. Nobody can be deprived of the jurisdiction under which he comes by law.

CLXVIII. Except for the case of a flagrant delict, nobody shall be arrested but by virtue of an order by a judge. . . .

CLXX. Nobody is allowed to enter the residence of an inhabitant against his will if it is not by virtue of an order by an official. . . .

ARTICLE 173. *The secrecy of the mails entrusted to the postal services . . . shall be inviolable.* . . .

CLXXI. Confiscation of property cannot take place for whatever crime it may be.

CLXXII. Every criminal judgment . . . must set forth the crime in all its details . . . and contain the articles of the law which determine the punishment.

CLXXXIII. Judgment in civil cases is to be motivated.

CLXXIV. Every judgment is to be pronounced publicly.

[The following section deals with the organization of the high court.]

CHAPTER VI—OF RELIGION

CXC. The liberty of religious opinion is guaranteed to all.

CXCI. Equal protection is accorded to all the religious congregations which exist in the Kingdom.

CXCII. All subjects of the King, without distinction as to religious belief, enjoy the same civil and political rights. . . .

CXCIII. The public exercise of any religion cannot be hindered unless . . . it disturbs public order and peace.

CXCIV. The salaries, pensions, and other advantages . . . which the different religions and their ministers enjoy are guaranteed.

CXCV. The King watches over the allotted sums . . .

so that they are not diverted from the use for which they have been specially earmarked.

CXVI. The King watches that each religion is not disturbed in the free exercise which the Fundamental Law assures.

ARTICLE 186. *The King watches that all religious communities stay within the limits of obedience to the laws of the state.*

CHAPTER VII—OF FINANCES

CXCVII. A tax can only be levied for the benefit of the treasury [and by virtue of a law].

CXCVIII. No privilege in matters of [tax] contribution may be granted.

CXCIX. The obligations of the state toward its creditors shall be guaranteed. The debt shall be considered every year for the purpose of promoting the interests of the creditors of the state.

[The following articles deal with mechanics of coinage, currency control, and auditing.]

CHAPTER VIII—OF THE DEFENSE OF THE STATE

CCIII. In conformity with the ancient customs, the spirit of the Pacification of Ghent and the principles of the Union of Utrecht, one of the first duties of the inhabitants of the Kingdom is to carry arms for the maintenance and defense of the territory of the state.

ARTICLE 195. *For the protection of the interests of the state there exists a military force composed of volunteers and conscripts. The law regulates the obligatory service.*

[Chapter IX deals with the functions of the public works system which, significantly, is primarily concerned with problems posed by water. The Waterstaat was then and is now an important branch of administration.]

CHAPTER X—OF PUBLIC INSTRUCTION AND THE WELFARE ESTABLISHMENT

CCXXVI. Public instruction is a constant object of the care of the government. The King will give each year an account to the States-General on the state of the higher, middle, and lower schools.

ARTICLE 208. . . . *education shall be free, except for the supervision by the authorities.* . . .

Public education shall be regulated by law with due respect for everybody's religious belief.

In each municipality the authorities shall impart sufficient public general elementary education in an adequate number of schools. . . . Private general elementary education which fulfills conditions of the law . . . shall be defrayed from public funds according to the same standards as public education.

CCXXVII. Print as the most appropriate means of shedding light [of knowledge] can be used without previous permission by everybody for the communication of thought. Nevertheless each author, printer, editor, or distributor is responsible for writings which will hurt the rights of either society or the individual . . . [This article does not exist in the present constitution.]

Chapter XI—Of Changes and Additions

CCXXIX. When experience leads to the recognition that changes or additions to the Fundamental Law are necessary, a law shall designate them with precision. . . .

CCXXX. This law is then sent to the Provincial [E]states which add . . . to the ordinary members of the Second Chamber an equal number of extraordinary members.

ARTICLE 211. *After the promulgation of this law, the Chambers shall be dissolved. The new Chambers shall consider that proposal and cannot pass the changes proposed . . . other than by two-thirds of the votes cast.*

CCXXXII. The Second Chamber . . . cannot pass a resolution . . . unless two-thirds of the members are present. Resolutions have to be accepted with a majority of three-fourths of the votes cast. . . .

CCXXXIII. No change in the Fundamental Law or the order of succession can be made during a regency. [This article does not exist in the present constitution.]

CCXXXXIV. Changes and additions adopted are embodied in the Fundamental Law and solemnly promulgated.

[The revised constitution has a number of additional articles which declare the remaining seignorial rights abolished, provide for pensions of members in the Chambers, and stress the temporary inapplicability of a few specific paragraphs pending final regulations.]

— Reading No. 10 —

TREATY BETWEEN AUSTRIA AND THE KING OF THE NETHERLANDS. VIENNA, MAY 31, 1815 [10]

Under the terms of this Treaty the Low Countries were united once more. But it was as enforced a union as that of the Burgundians or Habsburgs. Though this new union was based on a formal equality of the Belgian and Dutch populations, differences had become such that the countries were to break apart again within fifteen years.

✓   ✓   ✓

H. M. the Emperor of Austria . . . and H. M. the King of the Netherlands desiring to put into operation and to complete the dispositions of the peace treaty concluded at Paris, May 30, 1814, which is to establish a just equilibrium in Europe and to constitute the United Provinces in proportions which enable them to maintain their independence and assure to them the lands between the sea, the frontiers of France and the Meuse, but which have not as yet determined its [frontier] delimitations on the right bank of this river, . . . have resolved to conclude to this effect a particular treaty conforming to the stipulations of the Congress of Vienna. . . .

ARTICLE 1. The ancient United Provinces of the Low Countries and the former Belgian provinces, of which the

[10] Bn. Ch. de Martens and Ferd. de Cussy, *Receuil manuel et pratique de traités, conventions et autres actes diplomatiques* . . . (Leipzig, 1846-1857), III, 153-159. (This treaty minus the attached secret clause was separately signed by Great Britain, Prussia, and Russia.)

one as the other is within the limits fixed by the following article, form jointly with the lands and territories designated in the same article under H. R. H. the Prince of Orange-Nassau, sovereign prince of the United Provinces, the Kingdom of the Netherlands. . . .

ARTICLE 2. The [border]line marking the territories which shall compose the Kingdom of the Netherlands is determined in the following manner: it begins at the sea, and extends along the frontiers of France . . . [and] the Netherlands as . . . ratified and fixed by Article III of the treaty of Paris of May 30, 1814, to the Meuse and then along the same frontiers to the ancient limits of the Duchy of Luxembourg. . . . [Here follows a minute delimitation of the frontiers extending to the Rhine area.]

ARTICLE 3. The part of the ancient Duchy of Luxembourg included within the specific limits of the following article is likewise ceded to the sovereign prince of the United Provinces, today King of the Netherlands, to be possessed in perpetuity by him and his successors. . . . The sovereign of the Netherlands will add to his titles that of Grand Duke of Luxembourg and the capacity is reserved to H. M. to make such arrangements in regard to the succession in the Grand Duchy . . . as conform to the interests of his monarchy and his paternal intentions.

The Grand Duchy of Luxembourg serving as compensation for the principalities of Nassau-Dillenburg, Siegen, Hadamar, and Dietz [acquired by Prussia] shall form one of the states of the Germanic confederation, and the Prince-King of the Netherlands will enter into the system of this confederation as Grand Duke of Luxembourg. . . .

The city of Luxembourg shall be considered . . . a fortress of the confederation. The Grand Duke, however, shall have the right to nominate the governor and military commandant of this fortress with the consent of the executive power of the confederation. . . .

ARTICLE 4. The Grand Duchy of Luxembourg shall be composed of all the territory situated between the Kingdom of the Netherlands, as has been designated in Article II, France, the Moselle . . . the course of the Sure . . . and the course of the [Our]. . . .

ARTICLE 5. H. M. the King of the Netherlands renounces in perpetuity . . . in favor of H. M. the King of

Prussia the sovereign possessions which the House of Nassau-Orange possessed in Germany. . . .

ARTICLE 6. The right of the order of succession of the two branches of the House of Nassau by the act of 1783, the so-called *Nassauische Erbverein,* is maintained. . . .

ARTICLE 7. H. M. the King of the Netherlands . . . takes upon himself the charges and obligations stipulated in regard to the provinces and districts detached from France under the treaty . . . of May 30, 1814.

ARTICLE 8. H. M. the King of the Netherlands having recognized and sanctioned, under the date of July 11, 1814, as bases of the reunion of the Belgian provinces with the United Provinces the eight articles reaffirmed in the annex of the present Treaty, these articles shall have . . . validity. . . .

ARTICLE 9. A commission shall immediately be nominated by H. M. the King of Prussia and H. M. the King of the Netherlands to regulate all that is relative to the cession of the Nassovian possessions. . . .

ARTICLE 10. The present treaty shall be ratified, etc.

[In the separate and secret clause attached to this treaty the King of the Netherlands undertook to assume the debts and especially the mortgages contracted by the Austrian imperial government while the Belgian provinces were part of the Austrian Empire. Also attached as an annex were the Eight Articles, signed July 21, 1814, which served as the basis for the creation of a united Netherlands. The text is as follows.]

. . . H. R. H. the Prince Sovereign acknowledges that the conditions of the reunion contained in the protocol conform to the eight articles whose terms are:

ARTICLE 1. This reunion must be intimate and complete in such fashion that the two countries form one and the same state, governed by the constitution already established in Holland and to be modified by common accord according to the new circumstances.

ARTICLE 2. Nothing will be innovated in those articles of this constitution which assure to all the cults equal protection and favor, and guarantee the admission of all citizens, whatever their religious belief, to public employment and offices.

ARTICLE 3. The Belgian provinces will be conveniently represented in the assembly of the States-General, whose ordinary sessions will be held, in time of peace, alternately in a Dutch and a Belgian city.

ARTICLE 4. Since all the inhabitants of the Low Countries find themselves constitutionally assimilated, the different provinces shall equally enjoy all commercial and other advantages attaching to their respective situation . . . without any hindrance or restriction.

ARTICLE 5. Immediately after the union the provinces and cities of Belgium will be admitted to the commerce and sea-borne communications with the colonies on the same footing as the Dutch provinces and cities.

ARTICLE 6. The charges [incurred] before becoming common to both, benefits as well as debts contracted up to the era of union by the Dutch provinces on one side and the Belgian provinces on the other shall be the obligation of the treasury of the Netherlands.

ARTICLE 7. In conformity with the same principles the expenditures for the establishment and conservation of the fortifications along the frontiers of the new state shall be supported by the general treasury since it results from a matter which concerns the security and independence of all provinces and the whole nation.

ARTICLE 8. The cost of the construction and maintenance of dikes shall remain charged to the districts which are most directly interested in this part of the public service. . . . The undersigned . . . is charged and authorized to accept in the name of his august master the sovereignty of the Belgian provinces under the conditions contained in the preceding eight articles and to guarantee by the present act their acceptance and execution.

DECREE OF THE NATIONAL CONGRESS CONTAINING THE BELGIAN CONSTITUTION, FEBRUARY 7, 1831 [11]

The Belgian constitution was one of the most progressive of the nineteenth century. It compares favorably with the Grondwet of 1815, which was more pedestrian, cumbersome, and autocratic. The decade and a half that had elapsed between 1815 and 1830 had greatly accelerated the growth of liberalism and national self-determination. The difference between the two constitutions illustrates the changes that had come about by 1830. Yet in spite of these differences, the constitutions were sufficiently alike on many basic issues to demonstrate once more a common heritage as well as common goals.

✦   ✦   ✦

In the name of the Belgian People. The National Congress declares:

TITLE I—OF THE TERRITORY AND ITS DIVISIONS

ARTICLE I. Belgium is divided into provinces. These provinces are: Antwerp, Brabant, West Flanders, East Flanders, Hainaut, Liége, Limbourg, Luxembourg, Namur, excepting the relations of Luxembourg with the German Confederation. It is part of this law to divide, if necessary, the Territory into a greater number of provinces.

II. The subdivisions of the provinces can only be established by law.

---

[11] Great Britain, Foreign Office, *British and Foreign State Papers, 1830-1831* (London, 1833), XVIII, 1052-1065.

III. The borders of the State, the provinces, and the communes can only be changed or rectified by virtue of a law.

TITLE II—THE BELGIANS AND THEIR RIGHTS

IV. The quality of being Belgian is acquired, preserved, or lost according to rules determined by the civil code. . . .

V. Naturalization is accorded by the legislative power. The Great Naturalization alone assimilates the foreigner with the Belgian for the exercise of political rights.

VI. There is within the state no class distinction. Belgians are equal before the law; they alone are admissible to civilian and military employment apart from exceptions that may be established in special cases by a law.

VII. Individual liberty is guaranteed. Nobody can be prosecuted unless in cases envisaged by the law and in the form which it prescribes. . . .

VIII. Nobody can be deprived against his will of the jurisdiction of the judge to whom his case has been assigned.

IX. Punishment can only be passed or applied by virtue of the law.

X. The home is inviolable; visitation can take place only in the cases envisaged by the law and prescribed by it.

XI. Nobody can be deprived of his property unless [it is] for reasons of public utility [and] in the form and manner established by law and on condition of a just and preliminary indemnity.

XII. The punishment of property confiscation cannot be imposed.

XIII. Civil death is abolished; it cannot be reëstablished.

XIV. The liberty of religion, that of its public exercise as well as the liberty of manifesting one's opinions in all matters are guaranteed, with the exception of repression of offenses committed during the exercise of such liberties.

XV. Nobody can be restrained to concur . . . in the acts or ceremonies of a religion of which he does not observe the rest days.

XVI. The State has neither the right to intervene in the nomination nor in the installation of ministers of whatever religion. . . . Civil marriage must always precede nuptial benediction apart from the exceptions established by law, where it applies.

XVII. Education is free; all preventive measures are forbidden; repression of offenses will be only regulated by law.

XVIII. The press is free; censorship can never be established; cautionary bail cannot be exacted from writers, editors, or printers. When the author is known and domiciled in Belgium, the editor, printer, or distributor cannot be prosecuted.

XIX. The Belgians have the right to assemble peacefully and without arms conforming to the laws that shall regulate the exercise of this right, which is nevertheless subject to prior authorization.

XX. The Belgians have the right of association; this right cannot be subjected to any preventive measure.

XXI. Everybody has the right to address to the public authorities petitions signed by one or several persons. . . .

XXII. The privacy of letters is inviolable. The law determines the agents responsible for the violation of the privacy of letters entrusted to the mails.

XXIII. The use of languages in Belgium is optional; it can only be regulated by the law and only for acts of the public authority and for judicial affairs.

XXIV. No prior authorization is necessary to conduct the prosecution of public functionaries for [mis]deeds committed during their administration, except that which is enacted in regard to the ministers.

TITLE III—OF THE POWERS

XXV. All powers emanate from the nation. They are exercised in a manner established by the Constitution.

XXVI. The legislative power is exercised collectively by the King, the Chamber of Representatives, and the Senate.

XXVII. The initiative belongs to each of the three branches of the legislative power. Nevertheless each law relative to receipts, or expenditures of the state or the army must first be voted on in the Chamber of Representatives

XXVIII. The interpretation of the laws by authoritative means belongs only to the legislative power.

XXIX. To the King belongs the executive power which is regulated by the Constitution.

XXX. The judicial power is exercised by the courts and tribunals . . .

XXXI. The exclusive communal or provincial interests are regulated through the communal and provincial councils according to the principles established by the Constitution.

CHAPTER I—OF THE CHAMBERS

XXXII. The members of the two Chambers represent the nation and not solely the province . . . which has nominated them.

XXXIII. The meetings of the Chambers are public. Nevertheless each Chamber forms itself into a secret committee upon request of its president or ten members.

[Articles XXIV to XLVI deal with procedures.]

Section I—Of the Chamber of Representatives

XLVII. The Chamber of Representatives is composed of deputies directly elected by the citizens paying an electoral tax determined by the Electoral Law. . . .

[The following paragraphs determine the electoral laws and stipulate that only those could be deputies who met the following requirements.]

1. Each Belgian by birth or one having received the Grand Naturalization.
2. [Those] enjoying civil and political rights.
3. [Those] 25 years of age.
4. [Those] domiciled in Belgium.

[Article LI stated that the representatives had to be elected every four years and should receive a monthly allowance.]

Section II—Of the Senate

LIII. The members of the Senate are elected . . . in each province by the citizens who elect the members of the Chamber of Representatives.

LIV. The Senate is composed of a number of members equal to half of the deputies of the other Chamber.

LV. Senators are elected for eight years. . . .

[The following article regulates electoral procedures.]

LVII. The Senators receive neither salary nor indemnity. . . .

CHAPTER II—OF THE KING AND THE MINISTERS

Section I—Of the King

LX. The constitutional powers of the King are hereditary in the direct, natural, and legitimate line . . . in order of primogeniture and at the perpetual exclusion of women and their descendants.

LXI. In default of male descendants . . . the successor shall be nominated with the consent of the Chambers. . . .

LXII. The King cannot be at the same time chief of another state without the consent of the two Chambers. . . .

LXIII. The person of the King is inviolable; his ministers are responsible.

LXIV. No act of the King can have effect unless it is countersigned by a minister who for this [act] is alone held responsible.

LXV. The King nominates and recalls the ministers. . . .

[The following articles deal with the king's position vis-à-vis the army, and with his right to pass ordinances.]

LXVIII. The King commands land and sea forces, declares war, makes treaties of peace, alliance, and commerce. He gives as much information on these to the Chambers as the interest and security of the state permit . . . The treaties of commerce and those which will burden the state or bind individual Belgians have effect only after having received the assent of the Chambers. Cession, exchange, or addition of territory can take place only by virtue of a law. . . .

LXIX. The King sanctions and promulgates the law.

[Articles LXX to LXXVI confer on the King the right to summon, adjourn, or dissolve the Chambers, commute sentences, coin money, bestow titles of nobility, and confer honors. Other articles deal with succession and regency.]

Section II—Of the Ministers

LXXVI. Nobody can be minister who is not Belgian by birth or has received the Great Naturalization.

LXXXVII. No member of the royal family can be a minister.

LXXXVIII. The ministers have a deliberative voice in one or the other Chamber in which they are members. . . .

LXXXIX. In no case can a verbal or written order of the King remove responsibility from a minister.

XC. The Chamber of Representatives has the right to accuse the ministers and to arraign them before the Court of Cassation, which alone has the right to judge them. . . .

CHAPTER III—OF THE JUDICIAL POWERS

[Articles XCII to XCVI regulate the court system.]

XCVII. All judgment is motivated. It is pronounced publicly.

XCVIII. The jury is established in all criminal matters and for political delicts and [cases concerning] the press.

[The remaining articles deal with the composition of courts, number of courts, special courts, and the high court.]

CHAPTER IV—OF THE PROVINCIAL AND COMMUNAL INSTITUTIONS

XVIII. The provincial and communal institutions are regulated by laws. These laws ensure the application of the following principles:

1. The direct election . . . in regard to the chiefs of the communal administrations and of the commissioners of the government with the provincial councils.
2. The conferment on the provincial and communal councils of all that is of provincial and communal interest. . . .
3. The public character of sessions. . . .
4. The public character of budgets and accounts.
5. The intervention of the King or the legislative power in order to prevent the provincial and communal councils from exceeding their functions or hurting the general interest.

CIX. The editing of acts concerning civil status and the upkeep of registers are exclusively the functions of the communal authorities.

TITLE IV—FINANCES

CX. Any tax for the benefit of the state can only be imposed by a law . . .

CXI. The taxes for the benefit of the state are voted annually. . . .

CXII. In the matter of taxation no privilege can be established.

CXIII. Apart from the cases formally excepted by law contributions exacted from the citizens can only be in the form of taxes for the benefit of the state, province, or commune. . . .

CXIV. Pensions [and] gratifications charged to the treasury can only be granted by virtue of a law.

CXV. Each year the Chambers rule off the accounting law and vote the budget. All revenues and expenditures of the state have to be compassed within the budget and the accounts.

CXVI. The members of the Court of Accounts are nominated by the Chamber of Representatives and for a term fixed by law. . . .

CXVII. The salaries and pensions of ministers of religion are charged to the state. . . .

TITLE V—OF THE PUBLIC POWERS

CXVIII. The manner of recruitment for the army is determined by law. . . .

CXIX. The army contingent is voted on annually. . . .

CXX. The organization and prerogatives of the gendarmerie are the subject of a law.

CXXI. No foreign troops can be admitted to the service of the state, occupy, or traverse the territory but by virtue of a law.

CXXII. There will be a civic guard; its organization is regulated by law. . . .

CXXIII. The mobilization of the civic guard can only take place by virtue of the law.

CXXIV. The military can only be deprived of its grades, honors, and pensions in a manner determined by law.

TITLE VI—GENERAL DISPOSITIONS

CXXV. The Belgian nation adopts the colors red, yellow, and black and as coat of arms of the Kingdom the Belgian Lion with the caption: UNION MAKES STRENGTH.

CXXVI. The City of Brussels is the capital of Belgium and the seat of the Government.

CXXVII. No oath can be imposed but by virtue of the law. It determines its form.

.   .   .

CXXIX. No law, ordinance, or regulation of the general, provincial, or communal administration is obligatory before having been published in a form determined by law.

CXXX. The Constitution cannot be suspended either as a whole or in its parts.

TITLE VII—OF THE REVISION OF THE CONSTITUTION

CXXXI. The legislative power has the right to declare that there will be a revision under such arrangements as it may designate. After this declaration the two Chambers are dissolved. . . . There will be summoned two new ones in conformity with Article LXXI. These Chambers come to a decision in accordance with the King on the points submitted for revision . . . ; no change shall be adopted unless it musters at least two-thirds of the vote.

[The last chapter deals with transitory and supplementary dispositions, which include a variety of technical points. The Fundamental Law of August 24, 1815 was declared abolished.]

— Reading No. 12 —

THE LONDON TREATY, NOVEMBER 15, 1831 [12]

This Treaty, which came only sixteen years after that of the Congress of Vienna, sanctioned the separation of the Low Countries as that of 1815 had sanctioned their merger. Power policies again played an important part and a slightly reduced and much perplexed Belgium became the ward of the big powers. Signatories were Great Britain, Austria, France, Prussia, Russia, and Belgium.

✓   ✓   ✓

The Courts of Great Britain, Austria, France, Prussia, and Russia, taking into consideration the events which have occurred in the United Kingdom of the Netherlands since the month of September of the year 1830, the obligations which they are under to prevent these events from disturbing the general peace, and the necessity which arises from these events of making certain modifications in the transactions of the year 1815 by which the United Kingdom of the Netherlands was created and established, and His Majesty the present King of the Belgians participating in these intentions of the above-mentioned Courts, they have named for their plenipotentiaries [here followed the list of names] . . . who, after having exchanged their full-powers, found it good and in due form, have agreed upon and signed the following Articles:

ARTICLE 1. The Belgian Territory shall be composed of the Provinces of *South Brabant, Liége, Namur, Hainhault* [sic], *West Flanders, East Flanders, Antwerp,* and *Lim-*

---

[12] Great Britain, Foreign Office, *British and Foreign State Papers 1830-1831* (London, 1833), XVIII, 645-664. The official English translation is given here.

bourg, such as they formed part of the United Kingdom of the Netherlands constituted in 1815, with the exception of those Districts of the Province of Limbourg which are designated in Article IV. The Belgian Territory shall, moreover, comprize [sic] that part of the Grand Duchy of Luxembourg which is specified in Article II.

II. In the Grand Duchy of Luxembourg, the limits of the Belgian Territory shall be such as will be hereinafter described: [Here followed a minute elaboration of the line of demarcation.] . . . All the Territories, Towns, Fortresses, and Places situated to the west of this line, shall belong to Belgium; and all the Territories, Towns, Fortresses and Places, situated to the east of the said line, shall continue to belong to the Grand Duchy of Luxembourg. . . .

III. In return for the Cessions made in the preceding Article, there shall be assigned to His Majesty the King of the Netherlands, Grand Duke of Luxembourg, a territorial Indemnity in the Province of Limbourg.

IV. In execution of that part of Article I, which relates to the Province of Limbourg, and in consequence of the Cessions specified in Article II, there shall be assigned to His Majesty the King of the Netherlands, either to be held by him in his character of Grand Duke of Luxembourg, or for the purpose of being united to Holland, those Territories, the limits of which are hereinafter described . . . [Here were set forth the detailed stipulations regarding demarcation on both the right and left banks of the Meuse.]

V. It shall be reserved to His Majesty the King of the Netherlands, Grand Duke of Luxembourg, to come to an agreement with the Germanic Confederation, and with the Agnates of the House of Nassau, as to the application of the Stipulations contained in Articles III and IV, as well as upon all the arrangements which the said Articles may render necessary, either with the above mentioned Agnates of the House of Nassau, or with the Germanic Confederation.

VI. In consideration of the territorial Arrangements above stated, each of the two Parties renounces reciprocally, and for ever, all pretension to the Territories, Town, Fortresses, and Places, situated within the limits of the Possessions of the other Party, such as those limits are described in Articles I, II, and IV.

The said limits shall be marked out in conformity with those Articles, by Belgian and Dutch Commissioners of Demarcation, who shall meet as soon as possible in the Town of Maestricht.

VII. Belgium within the limits specified in Articles I, II, and IV, shall form an independent and perpetually neutral State. It shall be bound to observe such Neutrality towards all other States.

VIII. The drainage of the waters of the two Flanders shall be regulated between Holland and Belgium, according to the stipulations of this subject, contained in Article VI of the Definitive Treaty, concluded between His Majesty the Emperor of Germany and the States-General on the 8th of November, 1785. . . .

. . . So far as regards specially the navigation of the Scheldt, it shall be agreed that the pilotage and the buoying of its channel, as well as the conservation of the channels of the Scheldt below Antwerp, shall be subject to a joint superintendence, . . . that moderate pilotage dues shall be fixed by mutual agreement, and that such dues shall be the same for the Dutch as for the Belgians.

It is also agreed that the navigation of the intermediate channels between the Scheldt and the Rhine . . . shall continue reciprocally free, and that it shall be subject only to moderate tolls, which shall provisionally be the same for the Commerce of the two Countries. . . .

X. The use of the canals which traverse both Countries shall continue to be free and common to the Inhabitants of both. It is understood that they shall enjoy the use of the same reciprocally, and on equal conditions, and that on either side moderate Duties only shall be levied upon the navigation of these canals.

[Articles XI and XII dealt with road communications through Limburg.]

XIII. 1. From and after the 1st of January, 1832 Belgium with reference to the division of the Public Debt of the United Kingdom of the Netherlands, shall remain charged with the sum of 8,400,000 Netherland florins of annual interest, the capital of which shall be transferred from the debit of the Great Book of Am-

sterdam, or from the debit of the general Treasury of the
United Kingdom of the Netherlands, to the debit of the
Great Book of Belgium.

2. . . . Belgium engages not to admit, either at present
or in the future any distinction between this portion of
her Public Debt, arising from her union with Holland, and
any other Belgian National Debt already created or which
may be created thereafter.

[The following paragraphs and articles were concerned
with the mechanics of payments and state that Belgium
had been released from any other financial obligation
toward the Netherlands.]

XV. The Port of Antwerp . . . shall continue to be
solely a Port of Commerce.

XVI. Works of public or private utility . . . constructed wholly or in part at the expense of the United
Kingdom of the Netherlands, shall belong, together with
the advantages and charges thereunto attached, to the
Country in which they are situated. . . .

XVII. The sequestrations which may have been imposed in Belgium, during the troubles, for political causes,
on any property or hereditary estates whatsoever, shall
be taken off without delay, and the enjoyment of the
property and the estates above mentioned shall be immediately restored to the lawful owners thereof.

XVIII. In the two Countries of which the sequestration
takes place in consequence of the present Articles, the inhabitants and proprietors, if they wish to transfer their
residence from one Country to the other, shall, during
2 years, be at liberty to dispose of their property . . .
of whatever nature the same may be. . . .

[Subsequent articles dealt with further stipulations regarding the free sale of property and the abrogation of
specific taxation on such property.]

XXI. No person in the Territories, which change
domination, shall be molested or disturbed in any
manner whatsoever, on account of any part which he may
have taken directly or indirectly in political events.

XXII. The pensions and allowances of expectants, of
persons unemployed or retired, shall in future be paid on
either side, to all those individuals entitled thereto. . . .

[Article XXIII took up claims of Belgian subjects in
regard to nonofficial institutions.]

XXIV. Immediately after the exchange of Ratifications of the Treaty to be concluded between the Two Parties, the necessary orders shall be transmitted to the Commanders of the respective Troops, for the evacuation of the Territories, Towns, Fortresses, and Places which change domination. The Civil Authorities thereof shall also, at the same time, receive the necessary Orders for delivering over the said Territories . . . to the Commissioners who shall be appointed by both Parties for this purpose.

This evacuation and delivery shall be effected so as to be completed in the space of 15 days, or sooner if possible.

XXV. The Courts of Great Britain, Austria, France, Prussia, and Russia, guarantee to His Majesty the King of the Belgians, the execution of all of the preceding Articles.

XXVI. In consequence of the Stipulations of the present Treaty, there shall be peace and friendship between their Majesties the King of the United Kingdom . . . , the Emperor of Austria, the King of the French, the King of Prussia, and the Emperor of all the Russias, on the one part, and his Majesty, the King of the Belgians, on the other part, their Heirs and Successors, their respective States and Subjects forever.

XXVII. The present Treaty shall be ratified, and the Ratification shall be exchanged at London, in the space of 2 months, or sooner if possible.

In witness whereof, the respective Plenipotentiaries have signed the same. . . . Done at London, the 15th day of November, in the Year of our Lord, 1831.

— Reading No. 13 —

ULTIMATUM, AUGUST 2, 1914,[13]

Next to the Austrian ultimatum to Serbia, that of Germany to Belgium and the reply by the latter belong to the most dramatic documents relative to the outbreak of World War I. It was this ultimatum and its rejection that caused the German Chancellor to state that necessity knows no law (Not kennt kein Gebot). *As the result of the German invasion of Belgium, Britain entered the war, which was to assume a world-wide character.*

✦　　　　✦　　　　✦

Reliable information has been received by the German Government to the effect that French forces intend to march on the line of the Meuse by Givet and Namur. This information leaves no doubt as to the intentions of France to march through Belgian territory against Germany.

The Imperial Government cannot but fear that Belgium, in spite of the utmost goodwill, will be unable, without assistance, to repel so considerable a French invasion with sufficient prospect of success to afford an adequate guarantee against danger to Germany. It is essential for the self-defence of Germany that she should anticipate any such hostile attack. The German Government would, however, feel the deepest regret if Belgium regarded as an act of hostility against herself the fact that the measures of Germany's opponents force Germany, for her own protection, to enter Belgian territory.

In order to exclude any possibility of misunderstanding the Imperial Government make the following declaration:—

[13] *Belgian Grey Book,* in *Collected Diplomatic Documents Relating to the Outbreak of the European War* (London, 1915), pp. 309-311.

1. Germany has in view no act of hostility against Belgium. In the event of Belgium being prepared in the coming war to maintain an attitude of friendly neutrality towards Germany, the German Government bind themselves at the conclusion of peace, to guarantee the possessions and independence of the kingdom in full.

2. Germany undertakes, under the above-mentioned condition, to evacuate Belgian territory on the conclusion of peace.

3. If Belgium adopts a friendly attitude, Germany is prepared, in co-operation with the Belgian authorities, to purchase all necessaries for her troops against a cash payment, and to pay an indemnity for any damage that may have been caused by German troops.

4. Should Belgium oppose the German troops, and in particular should she throw difficulties in the way of their march by a resistance of the fortresses on the Meuse or by destroying railways, roads, tunnels, or other similar works, Germany will, to her regret, be compelled to consider Belgium as an enemy. In this event, Germany can undertake no obligations towards Belgium, but the eventual adjustment of the relations between the two States must be left to the decision of arms.

The Imperial Government, however, entertains the distinct hope that this eventuality will not occur, and that the Royal Belgian Government will know how to take the necessary measures to prevent the occurrence of incidents such as those mentioned. In this case the friendly ties which bind the two neighboring States will grow stronger and more enduring.

— Reading No. 14 —

NOTE TO THE GERMAN MINISTER, AUGUST 3, 1914. 7 A.M. [14]

The Belgian determination to reject the ultimatum and to uphold neutrality at all costs resulted in heavy personal and property losses. Yet the country, its people and government, set an example which reflected Belgian honor and patriotism. In the reply from the Belgian government to the German government this courageous attitude was foreshadowed.

✓　　　✓　　　✓

The German Government stated in their note of the 2nd August, 1914 that according to reliable information French forces intended to march on the Meuse via Givet and Namur, and that Belgium in spite of the best intentions, would not be in a position to repulse, without assistance, an advance of French troops.

The German Government, therefore, considered themselves compelled to anticipate this attack and to violate Belgian territory. In these circumstances, Germany proposed to the Belgian Government to adopt a friendly attitude towards her and undertook, on the conclusion of the peace, to guarantee the integrity of the Kingdom and its possessions to their full extent. The note added that if Belgium put difficulties in the way of the advance of German troops, Germany would be compelled to consider her as an enemy, and to leave the ultimate adjustment of relations between the two States to the decision of arms.

The note has made a deep and painful impression upon the Belgian Government.

The intentions attributed to France by Germany are in contradiction to the formal declarations made to us

[14] *Ibid.*, pp. 311-312.

on August 1, in the name of the French Government.

Moreover, if contrary to our expectation, Belgian neutrality should be violated by France, Belgium intends to fulfill her international obligations and the Belgian army would offer the most vigorous resistance to the invader.

The treaties of 1839, confirmed by the treaties of 1870, vouch for the independence and neutrality of Belgium under the guarantee of the Powers, and notably of the Government of His Majesty the King of Prussia.

Belgium has always been faithful to her international obligations, and has carried out her duties in a spirit of loyal impartiality, and she has left nothing undone to maintain and enforce respect for her neutrality.

The attack upon her independence with which the German Government threaten her constitutes a flagrant violation of international law. No strategic interest justifies such a violation of law.

The Belgian Government, if they were to accept the proposals submitted to them, would sacrifice the honour of the nation and betray their duty towards Europe.

Conscious of the part which Belgium has played for more than eighty years in the civilization of the world, they refuse to believe that the independence of Belgium can only be preserved at the price of the violation of her neutrality.

If this hope is disappointed the Belgian Government are firmly resolved to repel, by all the means in their power, every attack upon their rights.

— Reading No. 15 —

TREATY, MAY 11, 1867 [15]

This treaty, which guaranteed neutrality to Luxembourg and at the same time mollified France and Prussia, was another striking example of the interest of the great

[15] P. Ruppert, *Le grand-duché de Luxembourg dans ses relations internationales* (Luxembourg, 1892), pp. 600-603.

powers in the Low Countries. Similar to the London Treaty of 1831, which safeguarded the independence of Belgium, the treaty regarding Luxembourg was a compromise solution which could be upheld only as long as all of the signatory powers were ready to honor it. The Germans violated both treaties at the same time and for the same reason in 1914. The treaty was signed in London by Britain, Austria, Belgium, France, Italy, the Netherlands, Prussia, and Russia.

🖋   🖋   🖋

ARTICLE 1. His Majesty the King of the Netherlands, Grand Duke of Luxembourg, maintains the ties which attach the said Grand Duchy to the House of Orange-Nassau, in virtue of the Treaties which placed that State under the Sovereignty of the King Grand Duke, his descendants and successors. The rights which the Agnates of the House of Nassau possess with regard to the succession of the Grand Duchy, in virtue of those same Treaties, are maintained.

ARTICLE 2. The Grand Duchy of Luxembourg, within the limits determined by the Act annexed to the Treaties of April 19, 1839, under the guarantee of the Courts of Austria, Great Britain, France, Prussia, and Russia, shall henceforth form a perpetually neutral State.

It shall be bound to observe the same neutrality toward the other States.

The High Contracting Parties engage to respect the principle of neutrality stipulated by the present Article.

This principle is and remains placed under the sanction of the collective guaranty of the signatory Powers of the present Treaty with the exception of Belgium, which is itself a neutral state.

ARTICLE 3. The Grand Duchy of Luxembourg being neutralized, according to the terms of the preceding Article, the maintenance or establishment of fortresses upon its territory becomes without necessity as well as without object.

In consequence, it is agreed by common consent that the city of Luxembourg considered, in time past, from a military point of view as a Federal fortress, shall cease to be a fortified city. His Majesty the King Grand Duke reserves to himself to maintain in that city the number of troops necessary to provide in it for the maintenance of good order.

ARTICLE 4. In conformity with the stipulations contained in Articles 2 and 3, His Majesty the King of Prussia declares that his troops actually in garrison in the fortress of Luxembourg shall receive orders to evacuate the place immediately after the exchange of the ratifications of the present Treaty. . . .

ARTICLE 5. His Majesty the King Grand Duke, by virtue of the rights of sovereignty, which he exercises over the city and fortress of Luxembourg undertakes on his side to take the measures necessary for converting the said fortress into an open city by means of demolition which His Majesty shall judge sufficient. . . . H. M. the King Grand Duke promises furthermore that the fortifications of the city of Luxembourg shall not be restored in the future and that no other military establishment shall be created.

ARTICLE 6. The signatory powers of the present Treaty declare that the dissolution of the German Confederation having equally brought about the dissolution of the ties which united the Duchy of Limburg collectively with the Grand Duchy of Luxembourg to the said Confederation, it follows that the relation of which mention is made in Articles 3, 4, and 5 of the Treaty of April 19, 1839, between the Grand Duchy and certain territories belonging to the Duchy of Limburg, have ceased to exist and that the said territories shall continue to form an integral part of the Kingdom of the Netherlands.

ARTICLE 7. The present Treaty shall be ratified and the ratifications be exchanged in London within the space of four weeks or sooner. In witness whereof the respective plenipotentiaries have signed the same. . . .

— Reading No. 16 —

OUCHY CONVENTION, JULY 18, 1932 [16]

This rarely available document represents the first major effort to coördinate the economies of the later Benelux countries. This effort failed owing to the objections raised by the United States and the United Kingdom which protested the alleged violation of the most-favored-nation clause. But although the agreement was therefore never ratified, it constitutes a memorable step toward the future integration of the Low Countries. This step was all the more noteworthy as it came during the depth of the Great Depression when other states shut themselves off one from another.

🖝　　　　🖝　　　　🖝

His Majesty the King of the Belgians, Her Royal Highness the Grand Duchess of Luxembourg and Her Majesty the Queen of the Netherlands:

Taking their inspiration from the resolutions of the Assembly of the League of Nations and the concordant recommendations . . . as to the necessity for ameliorating the regime of production and exchanges and of expanding markets;

[16] National Archives, RG59, General Records of the Department of State, Decimal File, 1930-39, File 655.5631/25. Apparently this is one of the few copies of the Convention available in this country. The author wants to acknowledge here the help of Dr. Carl Lokke of the National Archives and of Dr. E. Taylor Parks of the Department of State in locating and using this document and the attached unofficial English translation. Ouchy is a suburb of Geneva, hence the term Ouchy Convention.

Convinced that the economic activity is seriously endangered by the more and more numerous obstacles encountered by international commerce . . . ;

Persuaded that the progressive realization of a greater liberty of exchanges is one of the essential conditions for the restoration of world prosperity;

Desirous of undertaking in this sense a concerted action, in which all states will have the privilege of participating;

Have resolved to conclude a convention for the lowering of economic barriers and to this end have designated as Their Plenipotentiaries the following [names are given here] . . . who . . . have agreed on the following articles.

ARTICLE 1. The High Contracting Parties [hereafter referred to as H.C.P.] undertake, in their reciprocal relations, not to make any increases in customs duties above the level of the duties existing at the date of the signature of the present Convention, nor to establish any duties not existing on that date.

The H.C.P. agree not to proceed to any increase of a protective character in their customs duties nor to establish any new protective duties with respect to the merchandise of third states . . . unless . . . the said states, by a new increase of the customs barriers . . . should cause grave prejudice to the H.C.P.

ARTICLE 2. The H.C.P. undertake to reduce progressively in their reciprocal relations, their customs duties in accordance with the following provisions.

The customs duties shall be reduced at the moment of the putting into effect of the present Convention by 10% of the rate existing on the date of the signature of the present Convention; the reduction shall be carried one year later to 20% of such rate, two years afterwards to 30%, three years afterwards to 40%, and four years afterwards to 50% of such rate.

The customs duties shall not be reduced below 50% . . . nor below a level corresponding to 4% *ad valorem* for semifinished and 8% *ad valorem* for finished products.

ARTICLE 3. The H.C.P. undertake not to apply among themselves any new prohibition or restriction on importation and exportation or any new regulatory measure which would have the effect of hindering their reciprocal exchanges.

They reserve, however, the right to bring to bear exceptions to this principle for the reasons enumerated below . . . [These reasons included prohibitions based on concern for public health and security, protection of artistic treasures, prohibitions applicable to gold, specie, paper money, and securities with the exception of measures of control of foreign exchange and of state monopolies. Under Article 4 of the Convention the H.C.P. reserved the right to require certification of origin or destination of imports and exports.]

ARTICLE 5. The H.C.P. undertake to apply to their reciprocal exchanges the unconditional and unlimited regulations of the most favored nation. [This was the issue on which the United States and United Kingdom attacked the Convention.]

ARTICLE 6. If a difference should arise between two or more of the H.C.P. on the subject of the interpretation or application of the present Convention . . . , the question shall be submitted . . . for an opinion by a permanent committee of experts to be established by the H.C.P.

If the Party concerned should be unable to agree to this opinion or if the committee should be unable to render a unanimous opinion, the difference should be submitted to the Permanent Court of International Justice.

ARTICLE 7. The present Convention is concluded for a period of five years . . .

For the H.C.P. which have not denounced the Convention [6 months prior to the expiration date] the latter shall remain in force on the same conditions . . . from year to year.

ARTICLE 8. Any other state shall have the privilege of adhering to the present Convention on an equal footing with the signatory states. . . .

[Article 9 regulated the ratification proceedings and Article 10 permitted the H.C.P. to declare that they were only bound as far as their European territories were concerned. A detailed explanatory protocol was attached to the Convention].

— Reading No. 17 —

PEACE TELEGRAM, NOVEMBER 7, 1939 [17]

In November 1939 a German invasion of one or more of the Low Countries seemed imminent. The sovereigns of Belgium and the Netherlands in their grave concern over the future of their countries exhausted every means at their disposal to halt the spreading of the war. While the well-intentioned but unrealistic proposals were cold-shouldered by the belligerents, for Germany was determined to conquer Europe, they represented the best traditions of international conciliation for which the Low Countries have generally stood in modern times. The telegram was sent from the Hague to the King of Great Britain, the President of France, and the Chancellor of Germany.

❦   ❦   ❦

At this hour of anxiety for the whole world, before the war breaks out at the Western Front in all its violence, we have the conviction that it is our duty once again to raise our voice.

Some time ago the belligerent parties declared they would not be unwilling to examine a reasonable and well-founded basis for an equitable peace.

It seems to us that in the present circumstances it is difficult for them to come into contact in order to state their standpoints with greater precision and bring them nearer one another.

As the sovereigns of two neutral States having good relations with all their neighbors we are ready to offer them our good services. If this were agreeable to them we are disposed to facilitate by every means at our disposal that they might care to suggest to us and in a spirit

[17] *The New York Times*, November 8, 1939.

of friendly understanding to ascertain the elements of an agreement to be arrived at.

This, it seems to us, is the task we have to fulfill for the good of our peoples and in the interest of the whole world.

We hope our offer will be accepted and that thus the first step will be taken toward the establishment of a durable peace.

— Reading No. 18 —

QUEEN WILHELMINA'S PROCLAMATION FROM LONDON, MAY 15, 1940[18]

This courageous and inspiring statement of the Dutch queen at the time of the gravest assault ever upon the people of the Netherlands is a lasting monument of Dutch fortitude. Not since the days of William I of Orange had there been a somewhat similar experience as well as a similar expression of determination to fight on, regardless of the odds, to ultimate victory.

✦   ✦   ✦

When it became certain that we and our ministers would be unable to exercise freely the authority of the State, we took the harsh but imperative step of transferring our residence abroad for as long as would be necessary with the firm intention of returning to the Netherlands when possible.

The government is now in England. It wanted to prevent ever being placed in such a position that it would have to capitulate. By the steps which we have taken,

[18] *The New York Times*, May 15, 1940, p. 3.

the Netherlands remains a full member of the community
of States and will be in a position to continue cooperation
with its allies.

The military command in the Netherlands will judge
what military measures are to be taken.

We ask all Netherlands authorities in regions occupied
by the enemy to do all they can in the interests of the
population. In the first place, keep order and calm.

Our heart goes out to our compatriots in the fatherland
who are experiencing difficult times.

The Netherlands will, by the grace of God, regain all
territory. Do everything in your power for the good of
the country, as we are doing. Long live the fatherland!

Remember calamities in the past centuries and the re-
peated resurrection of our country. That will occur again.

— Reading No. 19 —

KING LEOPOLD III'S DELEGATION OF POWERS, APRIL 15, 1950[19]

*In this strongly emotional statement the Belgian king
finally showed himself prepared to yield to public pressure
and open the way for the succession of his oldest son. He
had come to realize that at most he could assume the
rule over a deeply divided people. Such rule would have
perhaps meant the breakup of the country that his great-
grandfather had founded. In subordinating his personal
pride to the well-being of the nation Leopold showed a
patriotic sense with which he had generally not been
credited in the critical days of 1940.*

✓   ✓   ✓

My dear countrymen: It is with deep emotion that I
today address you. My first words will be to thank the

[19] *The New York Times*, April 6, 1950, p. 4.

nation for having shown me its confidence and having expressed the wish by the vote of its majority to see me resume the exercise of my prerogatives.

However, this deep satisfaction . . . cannot prevent me from thinking of those who on the 12th of March did not think themselves able to give me such mark of confidence [42.3% of the vote]. I must deduce from this if Belgian opinion in its majority believes it indispensable to put an end to the crisis that our institutions are undergoing, it is divided as to the solution for it.

During long weeks the crisis has been prolonged. . . . From diverse sides I have been told it depended on me to make possible a solution. . . . Faced with the gravity of current events, I do not think myself able . . . to forego the suggestion which is expected of me.

I ask all Belgians to hear it with the willingness to re-establish among themselves a settlement which will only be realized in respect for legality and with the sincere desire for loyal mutual understanding. . . .

In several constitutional monarchies, notably in Holland and in the Scandinavian countries, legal dispositions exist which permit the sovereign . . . to delegate temporarily power to the Prince Heir-apparent.

The adoption by Parliament of a similar measure . . . would give me the means for temporarily delegating to the Prince Heir-apparent the exercise of my prerogatives. . . .

I could evidently use this faculty only if this gesture were accepted with confidence by the great majority of opinion. . . .

I make to all Belgians an urgent appeal for union. I address myself in particular . . . to those who since my liberation have not ceased to uphold me with a moving fidelity.

I ask them to stick closer than ever to the throne.

To serve my country has always been my supreme goal. My most ardent wish is that my return to my country will be made under . . . [the symbols] of national unity and confidence in the future. May God protect Belgium!

— Reading No. 20 —

CUSTOMS CONVENTION, SEPTEMBER 5, 1944.[20]

The common wartime experiences caused the govern-ments and peoples of the Low Countries to draw ever more closely together. In September, 1944 the first major agreement on an eventual economic union was concluded. This agreement has been modified several times and aug-mented by a lengthy treaty, signed on Feburary 3, 1958, which now awaits ratification. But whatever modifications have been introduced since the Convention of September 5, 1944, the latter has remained the founding charter of the Benelux Union.

✓   ✓   ✓

The Government of Her Majesty the Queen of the Netherlands on the one hand;

The Government of His Majesty the King of the Belgians and of Her Royal Highness the Grand Duchess of Luxembourg on the other hand,

Desiring, at the moment of the liberation of the Ter-ritories of the Netherlands and the Economic Union of Belgium and Luxembourg, to create the most favorable conditions for the ultimate formation of a complete and durable economic union and for the restoration of eco-nomic activity, have decided to further these ends by establishing a common tariff of import duties, and grant-ing mutual exemptions from those duties, and to this end have agreed to the following articles:

[20] Secretariat-General of the Benelux Customs Convention, *Report on the Ministerial Discussions between the Neth-erlands, Belgium and Luxembourg* (Brussels, 1949), Annex 2.

ARTICLE 1

The Netherlands and the Economic Union of Belgium and Luxembourg shall impose identical customs duties on the importation of goods according to the appended tariff which forms an integral part of this agreement.

Apart from the duties provided for in this tariff, they shall be entitled to levy excise duties on alcohol, wine, beer, sugar, and tobacco, as well as any other taxes according to the system in force in the Netherlands and in the Economic Union of Belgium and Luxembourg; they shall reserve the right to modify the rates.

ARTICLE 2

No customs duty shall be levied on goods entering the Netherlands from . . . Belgium and Luxembourg and on goods entering . . . Belgium and Luxembourg from the Netherlands. The Netherlands and . . . Belgium and Luxembourg shall be entitled to levy entry duties on alcohol, wine, beer, sugar, and tobacco, and other taxes according to the system in force in their respective territories; they reserve their right to modify the rates.

ARTICLE 3

An Administrative Council on Customs shall be constituted; this shall be composed of three delegates of the Netherlands and three delegates of . . . Belgium and Luxembourg. The chairmanship of the Administrative Council on Customs Duties shall be exercised in turn by the principal delegate of the Netherlands and the principal delegate of . . . Belgium and Luxembourg.

The Administrative Council . . . shall without prejudice to the provisions of the annexed tariff propose measures aimed at the unification of legislative provisions and regulations concerning the collection of import and excise duties in the Netherlands and in . . . Belgium and Luxembourg and the adjustment of the latter to the provisions of this Agreement.

ARTICLE 4

The Administrative Council . . . shall be assisted by a Commission on Customs Disputes, composed of two delegates of the Netherlands and two delegates . . . of Belgium and Luxembourg.

The Commission on Customs Disputes shall make a binding award in the case of disputes concerning decisions taken in the last resort by the competent authorities in the Netherlands or in . . . Belgium and Luxembourg in matters of the application of the legal provisions and regulations resulting from this Agreement. . . .

ARTICLE 5

There shall be constituted a Council of Economic Union composed of three delegates from the Netherlands and three delegates of . . . Belgium and Luxembourg. The chairmanship . . . shall be exercised in turn by the principal delegate of the Netherlands and . . . of Belgium and Luxembourg.

The Council of Economic Union shall have the tasks:

    a. To give its opinions to the competent authorities in the Netherlands and . . . Belgium and Luxembourg on all measures which they might intend to take for the purpose of regulating imports, exports, and transit either with or without accessory duties especially by imposing restrictions of an economic character, such as licenses, quotas, special license fees, and administrative charges.

    b. To coordinate the above measures for the purpose of realizing a[n economic] system common to the Netherlands and . . . Belgium and Luxembourg.

    c. To administer the import, export, and transit quotas common to the Netherlands and . . . Belgium and Luxembourg.

    d. To give its opinions to the competent authorities . . . on all measures concerning production bounties or subventions which the Contracting Parties may propose to take.

ARTICLE 6

There shall be constituted a Commercial Agreements Council composed of three delegates from the Netherlands and three delegates from . . . Belgium and Luxembourg. . . . The Commercial Agreements Council shall whenever possible ensure the coordination of measures regarding existing relations with third states.

ARTICLE 7

The joint measures as envisaged in Articles 3, 5, and 6 of this Agreement shall be decided upon by the competent ministers sitting . . . for the Netherlands and . . . Belgium and Luxembourg. They shall be submitted by them for approval to the competent governmental or legal authorities.

ARTICLE 8

The present Convention shall be ratified and shall come into force eight days after the exchange of the instruments of ratification. It may be terminated at any time provided that one year's notice is given.

It shall in any case cease to be effective on the coming into force of the long-term economic union which the Contracting Parties propose to conclude.

ARTICLE 9

Pending the exchange of the instruments of ratification the Convention shall come provisionally into force as soon as the Netherlands and Belgian Governments are reestablished in their territories; either one of them shall have the powers to terminate it any time after six months notice has been given.

In witness whereof the Ministers Plenipotentiary . . . have signed the present Convention and have affixed thereto their seals.

BIBLIOGRAPHICAL GUIDE

LOW COUNTRIES, GENERAL

Geyl, Pieter, *Eenheid en tweeheid in de Nederlanden* (Lochem, 1946).

—————— *Holland and Belgium, Their Common History and Their Relations* (Leiden, 1920).

—————— *The Netherlands Divided* (London, 1938).

BELGIUM

Baudhuin, Fernand, *Histoire économique de la Belgique, 1914-1939*, 2 vols. (Brussels, 1944).

Cammaerts, Emile, *The Keystone of Europe, History of the Belgian Dynasty, 1830-1939* (London, 1939).

Dechesne, Laurent, *Histoire économique et sociale de la Belgique depuis les origines jusqu'en 1914* (Liége, 1932).

Garsou, Jules, *Les relations extérieures de la Belgique, 1839-1914* (Brussels, 1946).

Goris, Jan-Albert, ed., *Belgium* (United Nations Series) (Berkeley, 1945).

Kalken, Frans van, *Histoire de Belgique et son expansion coloniale* (Brussels, 1954).

Pirenne, Henri, *Histoire de Belgique*, 7 vols. (Brussels, 1900-1932).

—————— , *Les anciennes démocraties des Pays Bas* (Paris, 1910).

THE NETHERLANDS

Barnouw, Adriaan J., *The Making of Modern Holland* (London, 1948).

Blok, Petrus Johannes, *History of the People of the Netherlands,* 5 vols. (New York, London, 1898-1912).

Edmundson, George, *History of Holland* (Cambridge, 1922).

Geyl, Pieter, *Geschiedenis van de Nederlandse Stam* (Amsterdam, 1948).

Landheer, Bartholomew, ed., *The Netherlands* (United Nations Series) (Berkeley, 1946).

Smit, C., *Diplomatieke Geschiedenis van Nederland* (The Hague, 1950).

Vlekke, Bernard H. M. *Evolution of the Dutch Nation* (New York, 1945).

LUXEMBOURG

Herchen, Charles Joseph, *History of the Grand Duchy of Luxembourg,* 5th edn. (Luxembourg, 1947).

Putnam, Ruth, *Luxembourg and her Neighbors* (New York, 1919).

Weber, Paul, *Geschichte des Luxemburger Landes,* 3d edn. (Luxembourg, 1948).

BENELUX

Meade, James E., *Negotiations for Benelux; An Annotated Chronicle* (Princeton, 1957).

O.E.E.C., *Economic Conditions in Belgium, Luxembourg, and the Netherlands* (Paris, 1955).

INDEX

No. 1   MAKING OF THE MODERN FRENCH MIND
        By Hans Kohn

No. 2   THE AMERICAN REVOLUTION: A Short History—By Richard B. Morris

No. 3   THE LATE VICTORIANS: A Short History
        By Herman Ausubel

No. 4   THE WORLD IN THE TWENTIETH CENTURY
        By Louis L. Snyder

No. 5   50 MAJOR DOCUMENTS OF THE TWENTIETH CENTURY—By Louis L. Snyder

No. 6   THE AGE OF REASON—By Louis L. Snyder

No. 7   MARX AND THE MARXISTS: The Ambiguous Legacy—By Sidney Hook

No. 8   NATIONALISM: Its Meaning and History
        By Hans Kohn

No. 9   MODERN JAPAN: A Brief History
        By Arthur Tiedemann

No. 10 50 MAJOR DOCUMENTS OF THE NINETEENTH CENTURY—By Louis L. Snyder

No. 11 CONSERVATISM: From John Adams to Churchill
        By Peter Viereck

No. 12 THE PAPACY: A Brief History
        By James A. Corbett

No. 13 THE AGE OF THE REFORMATION
        By Roland H. Bainton

No. 14 BASIC DOCUMENTS IN AMERICAN HISTORY
        By Richard B. Morris

No. 15 CONTEMPORARY AFRICA: Continent in Transition—By T. Walter Wallbank

No. 16 THE RUSSIAN REVOLUTIONS OF 1917
        By John Shelton Curtiss

No. 17 THE GREEK MIND—By Walter R. Agard

No. 18 BRITISH CONSTITUTIONAL HISTORY SINCE 1832—By Robert Livingston Schuyler and Corinne Comstock Weston

No. 19 THE NEGRO IN THE UNITED STATES: A Brief History—By Rayford W. Logan

No. 20 AMERICAN CAPITALISM: Its Promise and Accomplishment—By Louis M. Hacker

No. 21 LIBERALISM—By J. Salwyn Schapiro

No. 22 THE ERA OF THE FRENCH REVOLUTION, 1789-1799: Ten Years That Shook the World
        By Leo Gershoy

No. 23 BASIC HISTORY OF MODERN GERMANY
        By Louis L. Snyder

No. 24 BASIC HISTORY OF MODERN RUSSIA: Political, Cultural and Social Trends—By Hans Kohn